MAGOR
FRAGMENTS OF HISTORY

MAGOR

FRAGMENTS OF HISTORY

DINA KENNEDY

HISTORY INTO PRINT

HISTORY INTO PRINT
56 Alcester Road,
Studley,
Warwickshire,
B80 7LG
www.history-into-print.com

Published by History Into Print 2010

A CIP catalogue record for this book is available
from the British Library.

ISBN: 978-1-85858-339-6

Printed and bound in Great Britain
by Information Press Ltd.

Contents

Foreword

HAVING COLLECTED a large amount of material on the history of Magor I realised that I ought to do something with it, rather than just let it pile up on the shelf and this little book is the result. It does not attempt to be a complete history; as will be seen it deals with selected documents, and stops short well before the modern village begins to develop.

I have tried to link the material so that the result is not too disconnected and to provide some historical background to put the individual items in context without overwhelming them in too much detail.

This is probably best described as an interim report on my researches since I hope to continue with the work, and to add much more material to my collection. I hope also that other people will read this and perhaps be inspired to follow my example and make their own contributions to the record of the history of Magor.

I have received help from many people whilst researching this history and I would like to thank particularly the staff at the Gwent Record Office and at the Public Libraries of Newport and Cardiff and the Library of Cardiff University. I am grateful to Peter Strong for advice and encouragement, and particularly to Robin for putting up with it all.

Dina Kennedy

CHAPTER 1

Looking back

THE EVIDENCE available for the history of a village is limited by what has managed to survive the accidents of the years, and the smaller the village the less material there would have been originally. Somewhere like Magor would enter the historical record only rarely, and a few passing references are little enough from which to build a history. However, I hope that by looking closely at such references; by looking at the documents in which they occur and trying to discover who wrote them and why they were written and also how they relate to the wider history of their times, we may be able to learn something of Magor and of the people who have lived here through the ages.

Before the nineteenth century we have very little official information about Magor and its people, since the first national census did not take place until 1801 and before that we have only a few parish registers which go back only to the middle of the eighteenth century. The few records that have managed to survive from earlier years are not necessarily those that were most important at the time, but only those fragments of parchment or paper that have not been destroyed by fire, water or insects, or thrown away as of no further use; and even when records have survived they often do not provide the sort of information we would like to have. For the very earliest times there are no documents at all and we have to rely on archaeology, and the few bits and pieces that have both survived and been found.

Looking at the present-day village it is not easy to imagine how it would have looked in the past. Even after only one or two years new buildings will become familiar and it is difficult to remember the scene before they existed; but with the help of such information as exists – and with a little imagination – we can make the attempt.

Let us first go back about sixty years and look at the village of the 1940's and '50s. Perhaps the most noticeable change would be the loss of most of the houses since much of the village dates only from the last few decades. The population at the beginning of the twentieth century was less than 500 living in around a hundred houses, and these figures did not change much for the next fifty years. A hundred years earlier when the first national census took place the population was only 268 and the number of houses probably around 50. There are also other major features of today's landscape that did not exist then. The M4 is a comparatively recent arrival, extending westwards from 1966, and indeed the first motorway in Britain did not open until 1959. The Severn would have looked very different without its bridges. The later of the two was opened in June 1996, and its elder partner is only thirty years older (opened 1966). The steelworks at Llanwern date from 1962, and the brewery at Magor from 1979.

Within the village also the road system has changed, the section of the B4254 bypassing the village centre was built around 1965, and other roads have been built to serve the new houses. However the appearance of the Square and its surrounding buildings, although there have been changes, would probably not have been too different. People could still use the railway fifty years ago as the station did not close until 1964, and there would have been buses and some cars, though not so many as today. If we go another 50 years back the cars would mostly have disappeared; when the records start in 1904 only one person in Magor held a driving licence and by 1914 the total was still only eight. Another fifty years back in the mid-nineteenth century and the railway too had only just arrived; it opened in 1850. Before that transport depended on horses, mules or oxen, or, of course, human effort. Nevertheless although self-contained the village would not have been too isolated since the Severn through the ages has been a means of transport rather than a barrier and contact with Bristol and Gloucester has always been important. The coming of the railway in 1850, the opening of the Severn tunnel in 1886, and much later the building of the two bridges, have continued this tradition. In fact travel by boat would have been preferred in earlier times when roads were unpaved, had deep ruts, and were probably impassable in wet weather. Not until the invention of a hard road surface by Mr. MacAdam [Tarmac] in the mid nineteenth century did the roads begin to improve.

The village had a school from 1856, although some education was available before this from the church, and from the Baptist chapel. There may have been a church in Magor from very early times but it is not documented until the thirteenth century. The chapel was founded in 1813, although non-conformist preachers were active in the area before that, particularly in the seventeenth century during the Civil War and the Commonwealth.

In the nineteenth century the village was largely self contained, with its own tailor, shoemaker, carpenter, smith, etc., though no doubt the villagers also traded further afield when they could and again cross-Severn links would have been important. Earlier still most households would have been self-sufficient, producing their own food and clothing and probably constructing their own furniture and even their houses, since these would have been of wood or wattle and daub, or even perhaps mud, since stone or brick were too costly. Most people would then have worked in farming or have been connected with it in some way and this would be true of Magor throughout most of its history, up to and even perhaps beyond the Second World War. There would always have been a need for specialist craftsmen such as blacksmiths, but they probably only used their skills when needed, spending the rest of their time growing food like their neighbours. Without mechanized tools most of the population had to spend almost all the time growing crops and tending animals merely to survive. Even time was different, there were no set hours for work, people got up when it was light enough to see to work and went to bed when it got dark. Before the fourteenth century time could only be measured by sundials or water clocks, and although the passage of time was also marked by the bells of churches and monasteries which rang for the regular times of service, these too varied with the time of year and amount of daylight. The calendar was different too; the modern calendar was not adopted in this country until 1752 although it was first devised in 1582. Since the new calendar had been introduced by the Catholic Church, Protestant Europe wanted nothing to do with it! When finally accepted by the government in 1752 it involved a jump of 11 days, and September 2nd that year was followed by September 14th. This resulted in riots with people angrily demanding their 'lost' eleven days back.

The development of the village would have been affected from the beginning by its physical surroundings; the higher land of Wentwood to the north dropping gradually to the Severn. However smaller scale changes in these surroundings would have taken place, some areas being eroded whilst in others deposition created new surfaces, particularly at the banks of the Severn where the boundary between land and water was infinitely variable and would remain so until relatively modern times when reliable flood defences were built.

Magor in pre-modern times would have been different in many ways. Smaller of course, and quieter; no planes, trains or cars, and no television or radio. It would have been darker too with no street lighting and few lights in houses. It would also no doubt have been much smellier with no facilities for sewage or waste disposal. Food would have been restricted to what could be produced locally and cooked on an open fire. We can perhaps imagine what life might have been like for the Magor villagers of early times but our 21st century village would be totally beyond their imagination.

CHAPTER 2

From the beginning

IN THIS chapter and the next I have had to cover a long period very quickly, since it has to be admitted that for most of that time there was nothing that can be described as 'Magor' or even 'Proto-Magor'. The most we can say is that there were people in this general area, and that we can know a little of them from the traces they left behind. Even when people began to settle down in one place rather than constantly move around in search of food; that is when they began to build and to farm, there is still very little remaining to show exactly where they lived. Gradually the evidence becomes more plentiful but it is not until the 12th century AD that the name 'Magor' first appears in the record even though we can be fairly sure that the beginnings of the village lie much earlier. Nevertheless we can look at such evidence as we have to see what we can learn from it, and also look at what was happening on a wider scale, at the sort of things that people in this area must have been aware of and affected by.

Humans first reached what was to become the British Isles during the last Ice Age. They had spread out from their original home in Africa over millennia, following the herds of animals that provided their food and clothing, which they hunted with weapons made of stone. They also used stone, wood and bone to make tools with which to skin and butcher the meat, to prepare the skins and also to gather wild plants and fruit to add to their diet. They also ate fish, shellfish, and birds; and would probably scavenge any dead animals they either found, or could take from other predators. As much of the world's water was locked up in vast ice sheets the sea level was much lower than it is now and what is now the North Sea and the English Channel was dry land. Men and animals roamed all over this vast area, retreating south as the ice sheets grew, and venturing further north again as the ice retreated. Britain was probably near the northern limit of their range and they have left only few traces of their presence. Locally there are only some worked flints found near Caldicot, and evidence that caves in the Wye Valley were intermittently occupied at this time.

At the height of the last ice age the ice sheets covered most of the British Isles, reaching well south into Gwent, and south of the ice there would have been a further area of barren land too cold for all but a few mosses and lichens, and completely empty of animal and human life. Gradually the ice retreated, only to return again for a long period around 10,000 BC, but after this there was a rapid warming, taking perhaps only about 50 years to reach temperatures higher than those of today.

By around 6,500BC the melting ice raised sea levels and Britain had become an island. What is now the Bristol Channel had previously been a wide plain, but here too the sea began to encroach on the land, drowning trees such as those whose remains have been found at Redwick.

For several thousand years the hunter-gatherer lifestyle continued but slowly changes began to occur. Groups of people began to exploit their surroundings on a seasonal basis, returning regularly to an area where they knew food would be available at a certain time of year. They also began to manipulate their surroundings, clearing woodland to provide grazing which would attract animals. Evidence for such clearance has been found at Goldcliffe, and also in the submerged forest at Redwick. We know very little about these people but they have left clear signs of their presence in the footprints preserved in the Severn mud at various sites, including Magor Pill.

Slowly, over more thousands of years, the herding of wild animals became the tending of domesticated ones and plants for fruit, seed or root were deliberately grown in small plots rather than gathered wild. Hunting and gathering would still have been important but gradually a more sedentary lifestyle developed. To this period belong the earliest of the great stone monuments, the chambered tombs such as that at Heston Brake, Portskewett. As time went on and farming developed so the social situation also changed as sufficient surplus was produced to support an elite.

Chiefdoms began to emerge capable of organizing a labour force to construct large monuments, and as the new material, bronze, began to supplant stone it was used to produce items intended for exchange or to show the wealth of its possessors, as well as for use. A bronze palstave, a kind of axe, was found at Knollbury Farm, Magor in 1950. A new style of tomb, the round barrow, developed and there are examples locally in Wentwood and elsewhere. On Grey Hill there seems to have been a more elaborate ritual complex of stone circles, standing stones and round barrows. This would have been a significant site for the surrounding area, and may even have been visible from the lower lands where Magor now lies. The standing stone at Llanfihangel Roggiett, even closer to Magor, may also date from this period.

As bronze in its turn gave way to iron, societies seem to have stopped building monuments of stone and turned their efforts instead to forts built on hilltops. These were also a very visible addition to the landscape. They were not only intended for defence but were an expression of the local identity and a focus for a defined territory. The hillfort at Willcrick is very close to Magor and probably dominated the whole of the surrounding area.

Throughout this time, people were exploiting the land, and have left traces of their presence. They continued to frequent the Severn Estuary and its margins, building wooden trackways to walk on, the remains of which have been preserved in the Severn mud. They also used the marshy lands bordering the Severn as pasture for their cattle, at least during the drier part of the year. Traces of some wooden buildings were found on Greenmoor when the Wilkinsons building was being constructed. These have been interpreted as sheds used when the cows were calving. Cattle hoof prints were also found there. No doubt these people also used the higher land beyond the marshes but they have left no traces there, at least none that have come to light in Magor. This may in part be due to the fact that many materials are only likely to survive in wetlands.

The Roman invasion of Britain, which began in AD43, met fierce resistance in south east Wales but eventually the Romans established a military centre at Caerleon and a civil town at Caerwent. These places have produced most of the evidence for life in the area during the nearly four centuries of Roman rule. However there is also some evidence from the countryside surrounding these major centres. The arrival of the Romans must have had a tremendous impact on the local people. Local leaders eventually adopted Roman ways and the people in general must have been affected even if they retained much of their old ways and beliefs. In practical terms the legionaries needed food for themselves and grazing for their animals, some of which must have been provided locally although some food and much of their equipment was imported from elsewhere. The presence of the legions on the levels is recorded on the engraved stone found at Goldcliffe which records the completion of 33 paces of a linear structure which might have been part of sea-defences or drainage works or might have marked a boundary.

There is evidence for a port at Magor Pill during Roman times, which may have taken over an existing site as late Iron Age material has also been found there. It was not large and most of its trade would have been local. There could also have been a nearby settlement although no remains have been found, but as any buildings would probably have been wooden they might not have survived. Most of the finds at the port have been of pottery and the various types suggest links by water to Somerset and also up the Severn to the Gloucester area. Some of the pieces of pot were made in Caerleon, and may have been brought to the port for onward distribution. The kind of boat operating out of such a port would have been suitable for use on the Severn and would also have been able to negotiate creeks at high tide. The remains of a boat of just this type, similar to others known to date from this period, were found in 1993 at Barlands Farm. It was a sailing vessel built of oak which dendrochronology has dated to AD283-301.

From the general area of this port the modern map shows a road leading in an almost straight line through Magor and on in the direction of Wentwood. It has been suggested that this represents the line of a Roman roadway leading from the port to the Roman road linking Caerwent and Caerleon, which at this point follows the modern A48.

Burials dating from the Roman period have also been found in the area, both to the west of Magor at the site of the Brewery, and on the other side of the village, in Undy.

The legionary presence at Caerleon lasted in some form for about two hundred years, and the associated settlement which grew up around would have continued to exist for some time after the legions left. At Caerwent, too, the civitas of the Silures remained a local centre long after the Romans left Britain. Although we do not know whether there was a settlement on the site that was to become Magor there is sufficient evidence to show that people were working and trading in the area, and it is not impossible that, somewhere under the present day village and now buried or destroyed by later building, lie the homes or farms of the people who lived here and tended their animals and crops whilst the legions marched to and from Caerleon.

Note on sources

Much of the information in this chapter derives from 'A Guide to Prehistoric sites of Monmouthshire' by George Children and George Nash published by Logaston Press in 1996, and from the first volume of the new County History of Gwent 'Gwent in Prehistory and Early History' edited by Miranda Aldhouse-Green and Ray Howell and published by the University of Wales Press in 2004.

CHAPTER 3

Romans to Normans

THE END of the Roman Empire did not happen overnight, in Britain or elsewhere, rather it was a slow withdrawal or rather diminution of presence that was not planned and which was probably unrecognised as such by contemporaries. It probably never occurred to anyone that the Romans and the legions would never return, after all they had been in Britain for nearly four hundred years and nobody could remember a time when they had not been in charge. For a long time people would have continued to look back to the age that had passed until, in the turmoil of the invasions and other disasters of what we call the dark ages, they gradually forgot and any memories that did survive became inextricably mingled with legend. Nothing or very little, either of history or legend relating to our part of the country survives from this time. We don't know whether there was any kind of settlement in what is now Magor, but both Caerwent and Caerleon continued to exist, for at least some time, and it seems reasonable to suppose that there were people in the area around, continuing to grow their crops and tend their animals as they had always done.

The dark ages are so called for the reason that so very little evidence survives to show what happened between the departure of the Romans and the emergence into history of the various kingdoms that existed in England and Wales before the arrival of the Normans. However, from the evidence that does exist, we can perhaps identify some of the events and developments that must have affected the inhabitants of the southern half of Gwent even though we do not know who they were or where they lived.

As the Roman presence was gradually reduced, local leaders would have emerged and established their authority over as wide an area as they could control. Any central authority that remained would not have survived the disruption caused by the various Germanic peoples, generally referred to as Anglo-Saxons, who began to arrive in eastern England from the middle of the fifth century. The newcomers gradually extended their settlements north and west, not without opposition, and Gildas, writing probably in the first half of the sixth century, refers to the rulers of several British kingdoms in the west of England and in

Wales. One of these, Aurelius Caninus, may have been based in south-east Wales but this is not certain. Gildas was mainly concerned with the sins of the people and their rulers, which he believed were being punished by the invasion of the pagan barbarians, and does not give many details. There are also a few relevant mentions in various sets of annals. In 577 the 'Anglo-Saxon Chronicle' reports a battle at Dyrham (near Bath) in which three British kings were killed and the Saxons gained control of Bath, Gloucester and Cirencester. This opened the Severn Valley to the invaders and would have been a matter of concern to the rulers of South-East Wales whether or not they were directly concerned in the battle. No doubt there were also conflicts, large and small, between the Britons and the Saxons which do not appear in the records. The traditional account of the origin of Pwllmeyric refers to a battle between the Saxons and the men of Gwent in about 620 and a Welsh annal notes, under the year 649 'Slaughter in Gwent' but doesn't tell us who was slaughtering whom. There are also references in all the sources to plagues, animal diseases and failures of crops which may have been connected to a deterioration of the climate during this time, giving generally cooler and wetter weather. Gradually the emerging kingdoms stabilised but continued to fight amongst themselves, allied with anyone prepared to offer support either Welsh or English, pagan or Christian. In 633 the Christian king of Gwynedd joined the pagan king of Mercia against the Christian ruler of Northumberland. In the following century Offa, a later king of Mercia, seems to have drawn some sort of stable frontier between Mercia and Powys, but also raided deep into Wales. Probably the raids were not all one way, hence the building of the great Dyke.

Relationships between Welsh and English may have begun to stabilise by the death of Offa in 796, but by then a new danger had appeared. The first Viking raid took place in 793, and they continued to raid, and to settle where they could, for most of the next hundred years until King Alfred began to gain the upper hand. There are references in 877-8 to a Norse army that had over wintered in South Wales and went from there to attack Devon. In 893 another army was driven out of Chester into Wales where they devastated and plundered as far as the Bristol Channel. Of particular danger to South Wales was the Norse settlements at Dublin and on the Isle of Man which lasted well into the eleventh century. In 914 Vikings from Dublin came up the Severn and plundered some distance inland where they managed to capture a Welsh bishop who had to be ransomed, for £40, by King Edward of England. The Dublin Vikings were still raiding in 1040 when the king of Gwynedd made alliance with them against his rivals in South-east Wales.

Rivalry between the kingdoms probably caused as much warfare as external enemies. In 848 a king of Gwent was killed by the men of Brycheiniog (Brecon) and in 878 the kings of South Wales sought the protection of King Alfred against the rulers of Gwynedd. Later, in 926 king Owain of Gwent is recorded as owing allegiance to King Athelstan. Such acknowledgement of overlordship was made by several Welsh rulers but it is not clear how much value either party placed on the relationship. Certainly it stopped neither side from attacking the other. In 1055 Hereford was burnt by the Welsh. In 1063 Harold Godwineson led a devastating campaign in south-east Wales to regain control of Gwent. Neither side was aware of the much greater threat that would soon cross the Channel from Normandy and eventually take control of much of both England and Wales.

William the Conqueror was crowned king of England on Christmas Day 1066 after his successful invasion and the defeat of the English king, Harold. Those who had accompanied him were rewarded with the lands of the defeated followers of Harold, but these lands were held from the king and he was determined to retain ultimate control.

In midwinter 1085 King William was at Gloucester and, as the Anglo-Saxon Chronicle relates:

> '... the king had great thought and very deep conversation with his council about this land, how it was occupied, or with which men'.

As a result of the discussion at Gloucester men were sent out all through England to make a record of the land and livestock held by everyone. The monkish writer of the Chronicle was rather shocked that the king should concern himself with such mundane matters:

> 'He had it investigated so very narrowly that there was not one single hide, not one yard of land, not even (it is shameful to tell – but it seemed no shame to him to do it) one ox, not one cow, not one pig was left out, that was not set down in his record'.

The survey was carried out surprisingly quickly, in less than a year, and although it was in many ways as thorough as the Chronicler believed, there were some areas in the more distant parts of the kingdom where the Norman lords were still establishing themselves and these were covered less completely. In the western borderlands William Fitz Osbern, a close companion of the king had been created earl of Hereford a few months after the battle of Hastings and he began building his massive stone castle at what is now Chepstow as a base from which to conquer the neighbouring Welsh rulers of Gwent. His castle was given the Welsh name of its site – Ystraigyl, the bend in the river, although the Norman clerks had difficulty with the name and it survives in many different spellings. The town that grew up around the castle was known as the Cheap Stow, that is the market town in old English, and this name was eventually attached to the castle also.

Gwent itself is not mentioned by name in the Domesday book, which is the name given by the natives to William's great survey by analogy with the Day of Judgement ('dom' or 'doom' being old English for judgement). However there are sections added to the surveys of Gloucestershire and Herefordshire referring to lands in the county. Monmouth and Caerleon are mentioned in the Herefordshire survey, and Chepstow under Gloucester, where it says:

> *'castellum de Estrighoiel fecit Wilhelmus comes'* – *'Earl William built the castle of Estriguil'*.

Domesday book was written in Latin as this was the only written language available. King William and his lords would have spoken Norman-French and their subjects old English (Anglo-Saxon) but although the pre-conquest kings had had some of their charters and law codes written in their own language, this practice had ended in 1066 and from then on Latin – the language of the church – was predominant, the more so since the church had a monopoly of education and only clerics (and monastics) could write.

Magor does not appear by name in the Domesday book, although there is the possibility (there is no proof) that it is one of the villages or 'vills' referred to in the Gloucestershire survey:

> *'Under Waswic the reeve there are 13 villages, under Elmwy 14 villages, under Bleio 13 villages, under Iudhael 14 villages. These pay 47 sesters of honey, 40 pigs, 41 cows and 28s for hawks. The value of the whole of this is £9.10s.4d.*
> *Under these reeves are 4 villages destroyed by King Caradoc.'*

These villages clearly still operated under the Welsh system of providing a render or food rent to their lords rather than doing manorial service as in England. A sester, or sextarium, was a measure of uncertain and variable size, reckoned at 32oz for honey; that is, equivalent to two modern one-pound jars. Honey was the only available sweetener at this period as neither sugar cane nor sugar beet was known (nor, of course, were saccharin or other artificial sweeteners). The pigs and cows were presumably to provide meat, and the money for hawks may have been for the purchase of birds for hunting, always an aristocratic pursuit, but may perhaps have been a contribution to the maintenance of the mews where the hawks were kept.

There are no indications of the amount of land involved, or the ploughs and plough teams available for their cultivation, as is usual in Domesday records. In England most of the land had been assessed in hides (usually reckoned as the amount of land required to maintain a household, but by this period an arbitrary measure derived from previous surveys rather than a realistic measurement) by the Anglo-Saxons and these records would have been available to the Domesday commissioners, but in Wales the system was different and hides were not used. Some of the land had been assessed in 'carucates' based on the amount of land a standard plough-team could plough in a year, which was the Norman usage, but these villages are still described in the old way as grouped together under their reeve.

The villages described as 'destroyed under king Caradoc' are probably those which suffered when Caradog ap Gruffudd retaliated after the invasion of Gwent by Harold Godwineson, that same Harold who was to die in 1066.

Note on sources
The Domesday Book includes information on Gwent under Gloucestershire and Herefordshire. A complete translation of the whole book was published by Penguin in 2002.

CHAPTER 4

The Monks

AFTER THE death of William Fitz Osbern his son rebelled against the king and lost his lands, which were held by the King, until they passed to another Norman family, the Clares, and from them to William Marshall and his sons.

In 1131 Walter Fitz Richard de Clare founded a Cistercian Abbey in the valley of the Wye, to the north of his castle of Striguil, and the grants to the new abbey included land at Magor. Much later, in 1307, monks from the Abbey travelled to Carlisle to obtain from King Edward I confirmation of grants to the Abbey as detailed in charters issued at various times during the intervening years. Between March and June of that year the required confirmation was issued but the abbey's treasurer had to pay 100 marks for the privilege, a large sum of money (A mark = 13s 4d).

There would also have been the costs, and the difficulties and dangers of so long a journey, but clearly they thought it worthwhile, and we can perhaps guess at some of their reasons. Probably they would have known that the King was ill, and in fact he died less than a month later. Moreover their patron Roger Bigod, earl of Norfolk, had died in December 1306 and since he was childless he had arranged with Edward that his lands would be inherited by the king's younger son, Thomas of Brotherton. No doubt the monks thought that it would be wise to obtain confirmation of the various lands granted to them in case of any dispute with a new lord. The charters that the monks went to such lengths to have confirmed have survived and give details of the various lands and privileges given to the monks by various patrons, including those in Magor. Such donations were intended to support the work of the monastery, but the donors did expect some return for their gifts in the form of prayers for themselves and their families. The more holy the source of the prayers, so they thought, the more effective they would be. For example Walter Marshall gave land to:

> *'St Mary, Tynterne, and the abbot and monks there, for his soul and those of his father and mother'.*

The charters were originally granted at various times between 1131 and 1306; however there is a lot of repetition, as donors confirm previous grants, so I will deal with all of them together here, regardless of date. I do not intend to cover the charters in full detail, only with such information as seems relevant to the history of Magor. The lands granted to the monks are not always described very fully, but some place names are mentioned which we can recognise as still existing and this gives us some idea of the areas in which the grants were made. Also, later records of Tintern's granges in Magor – which were known as Merthyrgerin and Moor-can help us to guess where the land in the earlier grants would have lain.

There are references to land 'in the moor of Magor' which presumably formed the nucleus of Moor Grange. Some of this was meadow which had formerly been held by Robert of Saint Brides, so that it had been in use before being granted to the abbey. However in other parts of the moor the monks were given leave:

> '*to make a dyke at their will, and in the dyke they may do what they will, and the water courses within and without they may order as they think fit*'.

This suggests that the monks intended to reclaim the land which may not have previously been farmed.

Merthyrgerin is also mentioned by name (or rather by several versions of its name – Martergeri, Marthirgery, etc.) and seems to have been an established settlement as there is a reference to:

> '*all that belongs to it with the church*'.

This was not the church in the village of Magor but a separate establishment, the 'martyrium' of Geraint, from which Merthyrgeryn took its name. This land seems to have come to the monks in exchange for some land which they were originally given at Wilcrick but we don't know the reason for the exchange.

There are also references to land at Scimoc, Scivau, Schiveau, Scyvioth, or Sciviot, all of which I take to be variations on the name that is now Skeviot; a farm that lies to the north of the village on the lane leading from Magor to Park Seymour (called Bowden's Lane, it is thought to be on the line of a Roman road from Abergwaitha to Wentwood, as mentioned previously).

Abergwaitha, the port at Magor Pill, is also mentioned, in a charter of Walter Marshall, who died in 1245. There was a mill there, and:

> '*the keepers and tenants of the mill of Aberweythal shall keep the watercourses running through the middle of the Alba Walda* (Whitewall) *and shall maintain the cut and sluice with a good lock so that the monks shall not suffer damage in their lands by the said cut or breaking of bridges or ways or any other harm which might arise*

by the default or malice of the keeper or tenant of the mill or by any other negligence of the donor's bailiffs and if anything of the kind occur, the person in fault shall satisfy the abbot and monks, and if needful shall be destrained by the steward of Strugull upon pain of 10 marks'.

This is a very specific and detailed section of a charter that is otherwise fairly general, and perhaps suggests that there had already been damage to the lands of the monks, resulting from the actions of the mill keeper, malicious or otherwise, and possibly with the connivance of the earl's bailiffs since their 'negligence' is mentioned. The Cistercians were often accused of greed in their accumulation of land, and in searching for unpopulated places in which to build their monasteries they were alleged to have destroyed villages and dispossessed farmers. Gerald of Wales refers to them as proverbially bad neighbours, but he had a grudge against them; and we cannot now know the rights and wrongs of the situation at Magor. However it does seem most likely that there was trouble and bad feeling between the monks and at least some of the local people. One possible cause is that the activities of the monks may have threatened their fishing and wildfowling practices. It is likely that the trouble was neither short-term nor trivial; it evidently warranted inclusion in a formal charter, and 10 marks would have been a heavy fine.

There is another specific reference in this charter that may suggest trouble. After saying that the monks should have *'a free road'* generally through all the donor's lands it goes on to specify one place, and one only, where this is to obtain. This is *'on both sides of the pond of Magor'*. The word for *'pond'* used here is *'vivarium'* which is usually translated as fishpond, or stew, that is an artificial pond holding fish for consumption rather than a natural feature. We don't know where this pond was but it may perhaps have been where the millpond would later be situated, near the centre of the present village, and so on the line of travel between the lands of the monks at Merthyrgerin and at Moor. Clearly there was some problem of access for the monks. Since the fishpond was most likely stocked for the benefit of the earl it is perhaps further evidence for ill-feeling between the monks and the earl's bailiffs as suggested above. The mention of *'breaking of bridges or ways'* may also be connected.

That the fishpond belonged to the earl is suggested by a reference to his 'garden of Magor' in another charter. In this Gilbert Marshall confirms the grant of his father, William, of:

'two floors (areas) in his garden (orto) of Magor, that is the last on the west side'.

The Latin word 'area' here translated as 'floor' can mean 'threshing floor' but it does not seem likely that there would have been a number of these in the same place; the phrasing suggests more than the two given to the abbey were on the west side and also implies others on another side. Another possible translation however, is 'vacant piece of level ground'. Could it be that William Marshall intended to establish a town at Magor, on the site of his garden there, and that the 'areas' were laid out as burgage plots awaiting tenants? This does not seem unlikely; R R Davies (Age of Conquest p 165) refers to 'a vigorous urban renaissance' begun by the first Anglo-Norman conquerors in the late eleventh century in lowland South Wales. Not all of these developments proved successful however, and although there are later references, in the second half of the fifteenth century, to 'burgages' in Magor, there is no other evidence of possible borough status.

In addition to this possibility, the mention of a garden and a fishpond suggests other ideas. Did the earl also have a house of some kind at Magor? I have found no information on this, and it is possible that the produce of the garden and fishpond were for use elsewhere. However there must have been local people to work in the garden, and also at the mill and in the port at Abergwaitha, and there would have been crops and animals that did not belong to the abbey which required tending. We know also that there was a church in Magor by 1238 (see next chapter) and I think that the existence of a village can probably be assumed even though we don't know how long it had been there, or whether it can be equated with one of the vills of Domesday book.

Note on sources
The Tintern charters – 'Inspeximus and confirmation of Charters in favour of the monks of Tintern' – are printed in the Calendar of Charter Rolls, Vol 3, pages 88-106.

CHAPTER 5

Magor Church and the Anagni Connection

WE DO not know when the first church was erected in Magor although the churchyard has a semi rounded shape which is said to be evidence for a very early date. The earliest part of the existing building is the tower which is thirteenth century. Further building took place up to the early sixteenth century, and much later extensive repairs were carried out by the Victorians. It is of course quite possible that an earlier building stood on the site but there is no evidence for this, although there is some re-used stone in the chancel which might have come from an earlier building. An early church could have been built in wood, and so would leave little or no trace in the archaeological record; it was not until the Normans arrived that the use of stone became widespread for the building of churches and of castles. A thirteenth century date suggests that it was the Marshalls who were responsible for the building, or possibly rebuilding, of the church in Magor. William Marshall the elder married the Clare heiress in 1189 and he and his sons, the last of whom died in 1245, were also responsible for much other building within their lordship. After 1245 the inheritance was dispersed between William's daughters and their heirs and there was no longer any central authority to organize such work.

The original dedication of the church to St Leonard might also be linked to the Marshalls. St Leonard is connected with Noblac, near Limoges, and he is the patron saint of prisoners amongst others. His cult became very popular in the eleventh century particularly among Crusaders who feared capture by the Muslims. Early in his life William Marshall was close to Henry 'the Young King', eldest son of Henry II; and it was at the castle of Martel near Limoges that the 'Young King' died in 1183, whilst in rebellion against his father. William was with him at the time, and it was to William that the dying prince gave his cloak bearing the cross of a crusader, and begged him to take it to Jerusalem, since he could not himself fulfill his vow to go on crusade. William did as he was requested, returning to England in 1186. Perhaps William prayed to the local saint at Limoges for protection against capture before beginning his dangerous journey and he would then remember Saint Leonard with gratitude after his safe return. Incidentally the church remained dedicated to Saint Leonard until 1868 when the dedication was changed to Saint Mary, for reasons unknown.

We met William's son Gilbert in the previous chapter when he confirmed a grant of his father. In 1234 he succeeded his brother Richard as earl of Pembroke and in 1238 he granted the church of St Leonard in Magor to the Convent of Saint Mary de Gloria in Anagni, Italy. Anagni is an Italian diocese in the hills to the southeast of Rome and had at that period close links with the Papacy. During the period from 1198 to 1303 four popes came from Anagni, and one of them, Gregory IX, had founded the Convent of St Mary there. Gregory was Pope from 1227 to 1241 and it was therefore whilst he was pope that Gilbert granted St Leonard's to St Mary's Convent. The reason for the grant, as Cal Hyland suggested in an article written in 1991, was probably bound up with the politics of the time. Gilbert, like his two elder brothers, was in dispute with Henry III over the King's reliance on his foreign favourites. There was strong suspicion that these men had been responsible for the deaths of William and Richard, the two elder Marshall sons, and Gilbert had only been restored to favour and permitted to inherit from his brother at the intercession of Edmund Rich, the Archbishop of Canterbury. The Archbishop also made grants to Anagni at the time and it seems likely that he and Gilbert were expressing their gratitude for papal assistance in their dispute with the king.

In 1239 Bishop Elias of Llandaff confirmed the grant to Brother Deodatus as the representative of St Mary de Gloria, but by 1252 rights in the church had already been farmed out, probably to the abbot and monks of Tintern, and by 1255 the arrangement was made permanent. It has been suggested that Deodatus, as the representative of Anagni, lived in what has been called the 'Procurator's House' by the churchyard but that building is of a much later date and it is unlikely that the church would have produced sufficient income for a permanent representative. The reference in the Papal register does not mention Tintern but they certainly held the rights later, and may have done so from the beginning, since they were much better placed than the Italian abbey to oversee the church and collect the tithes and other income.

There was an investigation into alien priories, that is those which had been granted to monasteries abroad, during the reign of Edward III (1327-1377). Edward was at war with France and strongly objected to any money, or information, passing into French hands – religious or otherwise. As part of this investigation the abbot of Tintern said that the abbey paid 20 marks a year for its rights in Magor church adding rather vaguely that sometimes it was paid to Anagni and sometimes to the pope. The Bishop of Llandaff, who was checking on his diocese for the king, added that he had been trying to find out about the 'House of Gloria' and where it was since he thought it might be in France, but without success. By 1385 however the king had been reliably informed that Anagni was in Italy:

*"which he reckons of his friendship, wherefore he has not reasonable
cause to take the fruits of the said church by reason of the war with
France"*

In 1395 money was paid to the abbey de Gloria by Italian merchants in Lucca
on behalf of Tintern. However by the early fifteenth century the Italian abbey
seems to have ceded its rights completely to Tintern.

To move forward in time, Tintern retained control of the church until after
the dissolution of the monasteries in the sixteenth century when the advowson,
that is the right to chose the priest, together with the revenues passed to the earls
of Worcester, later dukes of Beaufort, and remained with them until 1902, when
they relinquished their rights to the Bishop of Llandaff. The church was later
transferred to the diocese of Monmouth when that was created in 1923.

Note on sources
*The 'Calendar of Entries in the Papal Registers relating to Great Britain and Ireland:
Papal Letters vol. 1', gives information on the transfer of the Church to Anagni.*
* 'Llandaff Episcopal Acta 1140-1287' edited by David Crouch gives the confirmation
of the grant by Bishop Elias and the 'Calendar of Close Rolls 1385' gives information on
the investigation into Tintern as a possible alien priory.*
* The article by Cal Hyland is in 'Gwent Local History' no 70 1991 pp 5-9.*

CHAPTER 6

The Marshall Inheritance

THE MARSHALL family has already appeared in this record of Magor history, granting land to Tintern Abbey and rights in the church to an Italian abbey. William Marshall the elder became lord of Magor, and much of South Wales beside, when he married the heiress of the last de Clare lord of Striguil/Chepstow in 1189. He and his wife, Isabella, had five sons and five daughters and must have thought the family inheritance was assured. They could never have believed that each of their five sons would die in turn without children, and that in 1245, after the death of Anselm, the youngest son, and less than thirty years after the death of their father, the estate would have to be split between the daughters. Magor did not survive the partition intact. It was allotted to Sibilla who had married William Ferrers, earl of Derby, but as she, too, had died without sons her inheritance was further divided between her seven daughters. A little information about the village can be obtained from the various official listings of these transactions, but as the estates are divided and subdivided it becomes increasingly difficult to follow what is happening.

Magor was apparently a substantial part of the estate; in a later description of the lands to be partitioned Usk is given the highest value £107, but Magor comes next at £90, ahead of Striguil at £75 and Caerleon at £59. Unfortunately no boundaries are given for the various manors so we cannot tell how much land was included with Magor, however, since some of the land within the parish boundaries had already been given to Tintern, I think the 'manor of Magor' probably included some of the surrounding area as well. Clearly Magor was flourishing at this time; perhaps William Marshall had succeeded in establishing burgages within the village which were now yielding fees. The port at Abergwaitha may also have provided income, although as we shall see by 1327 it was described as being '*wholly deserted*'.

Sibilla's sister, Matilda, had married Hugh Bigod, earl of Norfolk and her portion of the estates included Chepstow, which led to the Bigod family becoming patrons of Tintern Abbey, as we saw in a previous chapter. They and their heirs also asserted a claim to lands in Magor. Twice, in 1281 and in 1316, after the death of one of Sibilla's heirs, officials investigating their inheritance found Norfolk's steward in possession and asserting that the lands in question were held from Chepstow. This was still in dispute in 1387 when Margaret, Countess of Norfolk petitioned Richard II to restore to her the *jurisdiction which she had over and in the vills of Magor, Radewyck, Porterton and Pulle*. An enquiry established that she had no such jurisdiction although she had for some time been trying to compel the inhabitants to hold their lands from Chepstow.

Another sister, Isabella, married the earl of Gloucester, Gilbert de Clare. His ancestors had been lords of Chepstow before the Marshalls, although he was descended from a different branch of the family. Gilbert and Isabella's grandson, also called Gilbert arranged with Maud, a daughter of Sibilla, who had inherited part of Caerleon from her mother, to exchange it, in 1269, for lands of his in England. This land in Caerleon he added to Usk and Trellech which he had inherited through his grandmother from the Marshall estate. Maud seems however to have retained her share of Magor since her heirs continued to hold land there.

Some of the various people who inherited from Sibilla appear in *Inquisitions post Mortem*. An *Inquisition post Mortem* is an investigation held on the death of someone who had held land from the king; and was held with the intention of establishing the rights and income which were due to the crown from that land. One such investigation was held at Magor in 1297 after the death of William de Mohun. He had inherited from his mother, who was Sibilla's daughter Isabella, land in Magor including pasture, arable land and meadow, with a house, rents from tenants and the right to hold a court. On his death the property had to be further subdivided between his two daughters, one of whom married John de Meriet. Another inquisition was held in 1327/8 on John's death and it found that he held:

> '... a fourth part of the manor of Magor in the Marches of Wales, including a pasture called la Grenemore and a port called Aberwythel now wholly deserted, held by the courtesy of England as the inheritance of Mary his wife of the king in chief by homage fealty and service of a sixth part of a knights fee'.

Abergwaitha, the port of Magor which has been referred to in earlier chapters, seems now to have diminished in importance perhaps because the land on which it stood had been eroded away by the Severn. The *'pasture called la Grenemore'* has also featured before being the area, now known as Greenmoor, where men of the Iron Age pastured their cattle, its use as pasture land had clearly continued through the ages.

Thomas de Rodberewe inherited through another daughter of Sibilla named Agatha, and in 1334/5 his inheritance included a house, lands and rents. He also had three free tenants, William Duraunt, William de Sancto Mauro and Robert de Gamages, holding property from him in Sudbrook, Undy and Rogiet. His *Inquisition* also gives a couple of place names, 'Chaumberleyneslond' where he held 24 acres of arable and 'Avenellesfe' which he held from the lordship of Chepstow. These two names also occur in a document of around 1505 which refers to 'the manor of Avenelleffee' which includes Chamburleyneslonde, and was 'within the lordship of Redewicke and Magor'.

John Seymour, who in 1358/9 held Penhow from the Lordship of Chepstow, also held Salisbury from the Lordship of Caerleon which suggests that Salisbury was not regarded as part of Magor at this time or rather that its inheritance had followed a different route. In the inquisition held after the death of Gilbert de Clare [son of the Gilbert mentioned above as exchanging lands with one of Sibilla's daughters] in the battle of Bannockburn in 1314, Salisbury is also held under Caerleon by the 'heirs of John ap Adam' but I have not discovered who John ap Adam and his heirs were, or how John Seymour came to hold the property. John also held some land in Magor jointly with his wife, Elizabeth. She may have been the daughter of the John Meriet mentioned above and inherited the Magor property from him although it is suggested in the inquisition that it came from Henry Fitz Roger who was descended from Sibilla's daughter Maud.

Another family who held land in Magor at this period, the de Knovils, seems to have inherited through yet another daughter of Sibilla, named Eleanor. However their property too, in the way that has become familiar, was eventually divided between female heirs. By the middle of the fourteenth century much of Magor must have been divided into a large number of small separate properties held by different families, although they all held directly from the crown. However if there were no heir to land which was so held it would revert to the crown, and I think this may have happened in several cases. In 1397 there is a reference to the lordships belonging to the king in the lordship and town of Magor and there existed later a manor called Magor Regis.

Of the *Inquisitions post Mortem* dealing with Magor that I have seen nearly half occurred in the years between 1352 and 1363 and I think that this is not accidental since in 1348 the Black death arrived in Britain and there would subsequently have been an increase in the number of inheritances to be investigated.

I have not described all the *Inquisitions post Mortem* that refer to Magor but the information in the others is of a similar nature, that is mostly names of people together with a few place names. On its own this is not very informative but it can sometimes, if it has been noted, be connected with other occurrences of the same names and so help to build up a more complete picture.

Note on sources

Details of the division of the Marshall lands are given in the 'Calendar of Patent Rolls 1364-1367'. Although this is about 100 years after the death of Anselm Marshall it does give brief details of who got what.

The individual Inquisitions are taken from the printed versions in various volumes of the 'Calendar of Inquisitions Post Mortem'.

CHAPTER 7

The Survey of Wentwood

IN OCTOBER 1271 the steward of the lord of Chepstow, William Welsh, called together the tenants of the lordship in full court to testify to the rights held by them in the 'forest' of Wentwood. A forest was not necessarily woodland. In law it was an area which had its own laws dealing mainly with the right to hunt deer and other game, a right usually reserved to the owner of the land. In practice most forests belonged to the king but the lords marcher had been allowed to establish forests for themselves along with other other special privileges. 'Lords Marcher' were given land on the border or 'March' between England and Wales and were expected to extend their holdings, and incidentally the King's authority, into Wales. Since they had to do this at their own risk and expense they were encouraged by being given rights and privileges beyond those normally allowed.

The record of the proceedings of the court has survived in several copies which vary in details but are on the whole fairly similar. At this time (see previous chapter) the lordship of Chepstow, or Struggle as the document has it (a version of Striguil; scribes often had problems with the spelling of Welsh names), was held by the earls of Norfolk and the present earl had succeeded his uncle the previous year. The new lord, Roger Bigod, was to take a much closer interest in his Welsh lands than his uncle had done and no doubt had in mind not only the extent of his tenants rights but also how far his own interests were restricted by those rights. The rights under consideration were those of '*houseboot*' and '*hayboot*'. Houseboot – or sometimes housebote – was the right to take timber for house repair and hayboot, or bote, the right to take timber for the repair of hedges and fences. These were 'common rights' but this did not mean that anybody could help themselves to timber in Wentwood, the rights were held 'in common' by a select and restricted group of people, and the purpose of the court was to establish who held these rights and what title they had to be included in the group.

Roger had of course inherited only a portion of the Marshall lands but it would seem that the whole of Wentwood, or at least the larger part of it, went with the lordship of Striguil. There seems to be no trace of any of the other heirs having any rights there, but the record of the court in1271 does not give any indication of the area covered by the survey and it may be that only part of the forest was under consideration. Since the earls of Norfolk did not receive Magor in the partition it does not figure largely in the proceedings but there are a few references of interest:

> '*The abbot of Tintern ought to have houseboot and heyboot to his abbey of Tintern and all his granges by charter*'

– thus presumably the granges at Merthyrgerin and Moor could take timber for use within the grange. The Tintern charters we looked at earlier state that Tintern had:

> '*...throughout all the donor's forests of Wales quittance of feeding and pannage and all their needs for housing and burning...*'

... which suggests that the monks had more extensive rights than are referred to in the 1271 record. Pannage is the pasturing of pigs in woodland where they would eat acorns, beech mast etc. and that the monks had '*quittance*' would mean that they did not have to pay for these rights.

> '*William Durant ought to have houseboot and heyboot at Redwick by charter*'.

I know no more of William Durant, but as late as 1566 there is a reference to a manor of '*Durant in Redwick*' which then belonged to Sir Thomas Morgan, and which was earlier known as 'Durantiscourt' so that William's name at least seems to have survived:

> '*Roger de St Maure ought to have houseboot and heyboot to his house at Undy and the same Roger ought to have houseboot and heyboot to his house at Magor by east common of Magor aforesaid called the Little Common of the one p'pte and the way leading from Aberweytha towards Wentwood by reason that John Rose held it and his heirs for ever*'.

The Abbot and William Durant held their rights 'by charter', that is they had written evidence for their claims. Other people in the survey held theirs 'by conquest', that is they had taken them by force from the previous owners who would probably have been Welsh. There is no mention however of how Roger came to claim the rights previously held by John Rose (who does not sound Welsh). It may be that the omission is accidental, but possibly Roger had in fact no legal right to his claim, and the lord of the manor had turned a blind eye to his activities.

Roger's house in Magor is '*by the east common of Magor called the little common*'. It seems likely that Roger's property was that known later as Castel Coch; certainly in 1314 a Roger de Seymour (who may be the same person or perhaps his son) held Castel Coch together with William Martell. If Roger's house was Castel Coch, then the East Common or little common is probably that area known later as Maes Bach. This also fits with '*the road from Aberweytha towards Wentwood*' since the road running past Castel Coch, now called Bowden's Lane, forms an almost straight line from Magor Pill towards Parc Seymour and Wentwood and as has already been suggested, may have been Roman in origin. The reference to Roger's land in this survey implies that Castel Coch was held from Striguil, and therefore that it was not part of the Lordship of Magor which was inherited by other heirs of William Marshall.

Roger Bigod III continued as lord of Striguil until his death in 1306 and an enquiry held after his death refers to '*A chace called Whitewoode, worth only 26s 8d because it was common all the year round*'. It is possible that Whitewoode is an error for Wentwood.

Note on sources
The Wentwood survey is printed in Sir Joseph Bradney's History of Monmouthshire volume 4, part 1, pages 146-148.

CHAPTER 8

Merthyrgerin and More

WHEN THE lord of Chepstow established his new abbey on the river bank at Tintern in 1131 the Cistercian order was only about thirty years old and was still bound by the ideals of its founders. These were particularly strict as they were a reaction to what were seen as shortcomings in existing monastic practices. The monks were to have as little contact with the outside world as possible; they had, therefore, to be able to provide food and clothing for themselves by their own efforts. However, as the monks were mostly occupied with the continual round of services laid down by their Rule, lay brothers performed most of the manual work involved. This sounds rather unfair to us but it did provide a way for more men to take up the monastic life since lay brothers did not need to be literate. As time went on however, the high ideals faded as they often do, and the abbey began to rent out the lands that had been given to them and to act in much the same ways as any other landowner, although this had originally been forbidden. As we have already seen the abbey also took over the revenues of Magor church although they would have had to pay for the services of a priest as monks were not allowed to perform these duties, probably because it would interfere with their monastic duties. These trends were accelerated, particularly after the ravages of the Black Death from 1348 onwards resulted in a severe labour shortage and it became increasingly difficult to attract lay brothers.

By the last half of the thirteenth century the tenants of the abbey were numerous and well established. Those living west of the Wye attended a court at Porthcaseg where money was collected and justice dispensed in the same way as at any manorial court. These were not like modern day criminal courts; they dealt with the administration of the abbey property and its relationship with its tenants. Some of the records of the Porthcaseg court survive and include references to Magor. The abbey's grange at Merthyrgerin had a mill and the abbey rented it to John Symonds. In 1302 he was in trouble for what the court called 'bad keeping'. He had pledged a total of seven and a half bushels, of flour presumably, to John, William, and Adam Ball. It is not clear what he had done wrong but maybe the mill did not produce as much flour from a given amount of grain as it should do, through either inefficiency or dishonesty. Flour was a necessity when everyone baked their own bread but only the lord of the manor could build a mill. Everyone else not only had to use his mill but also had to pay him for the privilege. This was no doubt resented and disputes related to mills were common. The Merthyrgerin mill was a water driven mill, on the St Brides brook, down in the valley below the grange buildings. There is no sign of it now but a mill in what was probably much the same position still existed in 1847.

The other reference to Magor in the court record for 1302 is to a change in the terms by which John Page held a tenement 'in the town of Magor'. He had previously paid one penny per year, but he was now to pay two pence per year and to build a house. Presumably the increase is because he will now have a house, or at least a new house, though he has to build it himself; 'tenement' does not necessarily imply a building, only something 'held' or 'tenented' from another person. Not only would John be paying twice as much for his tenement, but he also had to pay a shilling for permission to change the terms by which he held it. I hope he thought it was worth it! It is interesting that Magor is called a town, perhaps this is relevant to my suggestion that William Marshall might have intended to establish a borough at Magor.

The court at Porthcaseg dealt with abbey affairs in a fairly large area. Nearly two hundred years later, in 1493, we have the record of a court held at More Grange and dealing with just the one grange. Amongst the matters dealt with were some 'entry fines', that is a one-off payment made at the start of a tenancy in addition to the regular rent. In two of these the payment was 'two capons', that is not a monetary payment but one made in kind since capons are fattened cockerels rather than some obscure kind of coin. Jorum Ceys paid two capons for 12 acres of pasture which he was to rent for twelve shillings a year. The pasture was called Burdimesmead, and he had to repair the watercourse there. 'Burdimesmead' is described as *twelve acres of pasture lying next to Tadmead* and this latter is probably the land also known as Todmead or Toadmead which appears on the Tithe map of 1846 lying to the north of Redwick. Howell ap John of Llandevenny (the only obviously Welsh name) also paid two capons and was to pay rent of eighteen shillings and eight pence for a rather larger property. It included a tenement, here probably a house, together with gardens, and over 18 acres of pasture. The property was called Borland, and lay in the northern part of Greenmoor and is probably therefore the later Barlands farm. There is no mention of watercourses here, but Howell has to repair the hedges.

Tenants seem usually to have been responsible for maintenance and repairs, although some did not take their responsibilities seriously enough. The tenements of Philip Wilkins and John Melyn and the barn of Amice Bath were reported to the court as in need of repair and Jorum Philpot was in trouble over the repair of a dyke at 'Eriesex'. I am not sure where this was but it is possible that 'eries' should be 'erles' and Earls Reen; later Elves Reen forms the western boundary of

Redwick. Watercourses, and drainage generally, were of course very important on the lower ground where most of More Grange's property lay.

A larger group was in trouble for a different reason. Cattle had somehow got into Broadmead whilst the men were reaping but it is not clear whether their negligence permitted the cattle to stray, or whether they had deliberately allowed the cattle onto the land. Nor is it clear whether the men were reaping in Broadmead or whether they went there with the cattle. The court report says "trespass with cattle in Broadmead by reapers". Broadmead, by its name, is likely to have been meadow so possibly the men were reaping the hay and the cattle ate or trampled it before it could be gathered for storage. Whatever the exact circumstances it was a serious matter if the cattle had destroyed or eaten crops. The whole community depended on the production of sufficient resources to feed themselves and their animals over the winter, and starvation was always a very real threat. Broadmead is a name that still exists and is shown on the Ordnance Survey map, lying between Redwick and Whitson.

Between the two sets of court proceedings of 1302 and 1493 we have a different kind of record relating to the abbey grange at Merthyrgerin. By the end of the fourteenth century the grange was administered on behalf of the abbey by a bailiff whose accounts have survived for the period 1387-89 and these reveal in some detail the work of the grange. This grange being on higher ground, north of the present day village, had a mixture of arable land, for crop growing; pasture for animals, and meadows for hay. More grange, on the levels south of the village, had a higher proportion of pasture and meadow and less arable. At Merthyrgerin the crops mentioned in the bailiff's accounts are corn, barley and oats. Also mentioned are pulses – peas and beans – and onions. Work in connection with these crops includes ploughing, harrowing, spreading manure, hoeing and weeding. At harvest time there is reaping, binding and stacking corn; threshing and winnowing. Hay has to be mown, tedded, turned and stacked. Cattle are kept and a new byre for them is constructed. For this timber has to be obtained and sawn up, nails bought and plaster made and a thatcher employed to thatch the roof. It has doors for which a fastening has to be purchased. The byre includes accommodation for the drover, and the bailiff also records the purchase of candles for the use of the 'keeper of the oxen' in winter. Sheep and pigs are also kept and there is mention of a hen house and a stable. Other tasks include shoeing horses, mending ploughs, greasing wagons and repairing garden walls and the wall around the gate of the sheepcote. Purchases include leather to mend flails (used to winnow corn), iron for horseshoes, harrow teeth, and rope and grease. Some men catch a thief and hold him at night; they have to be provided with food. Other men are employed to 'clear rubbish from the way leading to St Brides'.

Much of the produce of the grange would have been for the use of the abbey, but some was sold. The bailiff records money received for pigs and piglets, straw and fodder, onions, pulses, ash trees, corn, barley and oats. Some meadow and pasture land was rented out, and rent was also received for 'crofts on the upland', 'a cottage by the bridge', and, from the vicar of Magor, for the 'rectory by Magor cemetery'. Was this possibly on the site now occupied by the ruin sometimes called the 'Procurators House'? The existing building is thought to have been a sixteenth century Priests House but this rectory may have been its predecessor.

An archaeological investigation in 1971-2 at Upper Grange Farm found evidence of medieval buildings, considered likely to have formed part of the grange. There was no pottery or other evidence of human occupation so that these buildings were probably for agricultural rather than domestic purposes.

Note on sources
The information in this chapter is taken from the article by D H Williams, 'Tintern Abbey: its economic history' in The Monmouthshire Antiquary for 1965.

The archaeological investigation at Merthyrgerin is reported in Archaeologica Cambrensis 1974, 'Merthyrgerin: a grange of Tintern' by L N Parkes and P V Webster.

CHAPTER 9

Law and Disorder

THE LORD of a manor, even when that 'lord' was a religious institution, held courts for the tenants of that manor, as we saw in the last chapter, but there were other courts too which have left records giving some glimpses of life in Magor.

In 1415 John Mowbray, earl marshall, ordered 'sessions in eyre', that is courts held by justices travelling around, to be held in all his Welsh lands including Chepstow. John was the great-grandson of Margaret, countess of Norfolk who had earlier, as we saw, tried to assert her authority over Magor. Margaret died in 1399 and her heir was John's brother Thomas, but he was executed in 1405 after taking part in a rebellion against Henry IV. John was then still a minor and did not come into his inheritance until 1413, and it is possible that he wished to check on the administration of his estates in the years since the death of his great-grandmother. In May 1415, amongst other matters, fifteen men accused of felony and other offences were summoned to appear before the justices at Chepstow. They did not appear and the sheriff was therefore ordered to arrest them, but he reported that they could not be found. Consequently the court declared them outlawed. We do not know the details of their offences, nor all of their names, but one of them is described as 'John Bridde of Magor' and it so happens that we know a little about John Bridde from other sources.

About three years before the court at Chepstow the monks of Moor Grange in Magor recorded the payment of 11 shillings to John Bridde for 'newly making a weir called Erlisgout'. A '*gout*' is part of the drainage system, a kind of sluice to regulate the flow of water and prevent the incoming tide from flooding up the reen. Erlisgout was presumably part of the Erlis or Erles Reen which lay to the west of Redwick [now called Elver reen]. Its construction and maintenance was a matter of some importance and the monks must have thought John a sufficiently capable and responsible person to be entrusted with the work. This does not altogether fit with the 'outlaw' of the Chepstow court.

Around twenty years later there are a number of references to John Bridde of Magor in deeds relating to the lease of land. In 1434 and 1439 he is one of the witnesses to a deed, and in the latter case one of the boundaries of the land involved is 'the tenement of John Bridd'. Later, in 1448, he receives land himself, two acres of arable land in 'the field of Magor'. This would have been part of the common field of Magor where individuals were allocated strips in the large open field or fields of the village. John's land is described in the deed; one acre lay in 'Leybutt Sherde'which I cannot identify although there are references in the eighteenth century to 'Bushhay' and 'Buttay' which may be related. The other acre lay near the 'Marlepitt', marl being soil formed of a mixture of clay and lime which was used as a fertilizer.

There are frequent references to the marlepitt or marlepitt field which seems, at least by the beginning of the 19th century, to have been another name for the Lower Field in Magor which stretched from the village along the south-west side of the Newport Road. Here too John Bridde appears as a respected member of the community, clearly his outlaw status did not affect his later life. It is perhaps possible that the reason he and the others did not appear before the court was that they saw it as a further attempt by the lord of Chepstow to include Magor in his lordship, and that they did not accept his authority. In looking at the records of court proceedings such as that involving John Bridde we do not usually have enough information to know what really happened, and often we have only one side of the story.

In an age when all men were expected to follow their lord to war when required, and when they had to be prepared to act in defence of themselves, their families and their property since there was no official force to do so on their behalf, it is likely that contemporary attitudes to men who took the law into their own hands were very different to those of later times. Violent action either official or unofficial was probably much more a part of ordinary life. Those attending the court which outlawed John Bridde in 1415 would have experienced the turmoil attending the revolt of Owain Glyndwr, during which, only ten years earlier, there had been battles in Gwent at Grosmont and at Usk. The Hundred Years War with France would continue for another forty years; indeed in the October following the court at Chepstow, Henry V and his forces, including many Welshmen, fought and won the battle of Agincourt. While the king and the army were in France it was necessary to provide for security at home and Henry had written, in May 1415 at the same time as the court was held in Chepstow, to the bishops demanding that they assemble a force from their clergy:

> '...for the secure keeping and defence of the realm and of the English church'.

The bishop of Llandaff had visited various parts of his diocese to carry out the king's orders and at Magor he found 55 suitable men from the deanery of Netherwent.

Another example of local disorder dates from 1476. At a court held at Machen a number of men were accused of abducting Roger Coys, the king's bailiff of

Netherwent, from the Lordship of Magor; of robbing him of money belonging both to himself and to the king, and of keeping him prisoner in Newport. Three men were named in the report, two of them were acquitted and the third did not appear, leaving us wondering what actually did happen. It is perhaps not surprising that this too was a violent period. The war with France may have ended but 1450 saw the beginning of the Wars of the Roses. No doubt the ordinary people, in Magor as elsewhere, kept their heads down and tried to get on with their lives as best they could but they cannot have escaped altogether. This would apply particularly as from 1462 Magor formed part of the lands granted by Edward IV to William Herbert, earl of Pembroke, and his tenants there would be expected to follow him to war. William Herbert was killed at the battle of Edgecote in 1469 and, as his heir was a child, it would seem from the description of Roger Coys as 'the king's bailiff' that Netherwent at least was being administered by Edward IV, although the king may have retained control of the parts of Magor held directly from the crown.

After Henry Tudor came to power in 1485, Magor passed under the control of his uncle Jasper, now Duke of Bedford, and in 1490 an agreement was signed concerning the government of the Duke's Marcher lordships. These included, amongst others, Newport, Caldicot and Magor. Such an agreement might suggest that the area was particularly lawless, but alternatively there may have been continuing opposition to the rule of Henry VII in an area where the Yorkist party had been important. There are no details given in the agreement, only references to:

> *"the subduyng of grete robberies, murdres and other offences there used byfore this tyme".*

Some of the problems experienced in maintaining law and order in the Marches derived from the aftermath of the Norman Conquest. The March was then very much on the frontier of a recently conquered country, and those lords entrusted with the extension of the conquest were given a greater amount of power in their territories than was the case elsewhere. Since then the crown had been trying, with little success, to reduce the independence of the Marcher lords and those same lords were determined to hold on to as much power as possible. The Council in the Marches of Wales was one body set up to try to control the area, in much the same way as Henry VII's agreement with Jasper Tudor. In 1534 the President of this Council was the bishop of Coventry and Lichfield, Rowland Lee. A letter he wrote to Thomas Cromwell, Henry VIII's minister has often been quoted as showing the extent of the lawlessness of the March, and since Magor is mentioned in the letter the village has gained, unfairly I think, a particularly bad reputation. The bishop is concerned by the number of criminals being protected by Walter Herbert in 'the king's lordship of Magor'. Certainly a number of crimes were committed by men who were Walter's friends or relatives. On the other hand the accusations, true or false, are probably part of an ongoing feud between the Herberts and the Morgans which in 1533 erupted in rioting in Newport during which one man died. Walter Herbert was certainly the steward in Magor of the earl of Worcester, who had inherited from his mother, the grand-daughter and heiress of the William Herbert who died at Edgecote, and who also apparently leased the crown property in Magor. Walter himself lived at St Julians outside Newport however, and since only six men, out of 43 mentioned in the letter, are said to have been directly connected with Magor it does not seem that Magor was any worse than any other place.

Members of the Morgan family, like the Herberts widespread in Gwent, were implicated in another court case during the reign of Queen Elizabeth. The case was brought in the Court of Star Chamber by William David of Penhow against James Morgan of Magor and several others. It is not altogether clear what happened but there seems to have been a dispute about a mare bought at Chepstow market, and on the way to the assizes, where the case was to be dealt with, William was assaulted by Morgan and his companions. There was a further assault on the way back and he was *'left for dead in an alehouse in Penhow'*. I don't know whether this second assault took place in the alehouse or whether his assailants considerately took him there after they had finished! The accusations were the more serious since James Morgan was the high constable of Caldicot and his companions were petty constables. One of those companions, William Morgan of Magor, himself brought a case to the court of Star Chamber in which he accused Walter ap Powell of Magor and his wife Blanche together with other people of *'assaults at Magor upon the complainant and upon divers others'* – no further details are given. Despite my defence, above, of Magor's reputation it does seem to have been a somewhat violent place, but again it was probably no more so than other places.

During the same period records have survived of the Quarter Sessions held in Gwent which have a few references to Magor. At the various Sessions fines were levied on jurors who failed to attend. These include Walter ap Howell of Magor, John Rees and Adam ap Jenkyn of Undy, Richard Wyllym, David ap Jenkin, Lawrence John Lewis and John Williams of Redwick, and Lambroth Robnet of St Brides. At Abergavenny Quarter Session in 1577 James Williams and Henry Yoroth of Redwick and John Goseling of Magor were each fined two shillings for selling ale without the licence of the justices.

In chapter 10 we saw reapers in trouble when cattle got into Broadmead. In the same 1577 Sessions mentioned above Howell Jeyn Davy, yeoman, and two labourers named John Watkins and William Ogans, all of Redwick, were accused of trespassing in Broadmead, which then belonged to William Herbert of Colbroke, where they cut hay and carried it away.

Also in 1577 William George, a labourer of Undy, was in Monmouth gaol accused of the murder of Watkin Howell by striking him on the head with a stone. It is possible that Watkin Howell is the same person as the Walter ap Powell of

Magor fined for non-attendance at the Quarter Sessions that same year, the names are very similar.

Note on sources

In 'Marcher Lordships of South Wales by T B Pugh.' the court at Chepstow is mentioned on page15 and that at Machen on page 26.

I have written in more detail about Walter Herbert and the accusations made by Bishop Rowland Lee in 'A den of thieves and murderers? Magor in the 1530s' published in 'Gwent Local History' No 87 1999.

Details of the Star Chamber cases are taken from 'Catalogue of Star Chamber Proceedings related to Wales' published in 1929.

Information on the Gwent Quarter Sessions is from 'Law and Disorder in Tudor Monmouthshire' by Ben Howell published by Merton Priory Press in 1995.

CHAPTER 10

Clerical Gentlemen

AT SOME time in the late 13th or early 14th century the bishop of Llandaff wrote a letter referring to Magor. It is quite short so I will quote it in full. The writer:

> *'appeals on behalf of Richard vicar of Magor and his poor parishioners that the addressee will order the escheator and those intendant to him in the parts of Magor to allow the said Richard and his parishioners to have that part which belongs to them of the fruits of certain lands, which they have cultivated, and which were handed over to them by the bailiffs of the Earl of Gloucester, who at the time were keepers of the said land. The bishop reminds the addressee that the keepership of which he has spoken is demised to the bishop at farm until the boy becomes of age. [usque etatem pueri]'*

This is a typically frustrating and incomplete bit of evidence as the letter is written in Latin, the names of the bishop and his correspondent are not mentioned and the letter is not dated. Added to this is the fact that the letter has disappeared! It was printed in a book published in 1935 but a later author could not trace it. A check on the bishops of Llandaff of the period throws a little light on the circumstances since between 1287 and 1296 the see was vacant. The fact that the land was formerly in the hands of the earl of Gloucester's bailiffs but is now controlled by an escheator suggests that the earl had recently died. Since all land technically belonged to the king, it reverted to him when the holder of the land died, and an escheator was required to establish the extent of the holdings and who should inherit – usually the heir of the previous holder but this was not automatic. In this case it seems that the heir was not of age since guardianship has been *'demised to the bishop at farm'*, that is the bishop has paid to have control of the heir and his lands, and of course the income from those lands, until the boy is of age. The earl of Gloucester, that Gilbert de Clare whom we met in chapter 6 gaining part of Caerleon by exchange, did indeed die in 1295 leaving a son, also named Gilbert aged 4 or 5. Although Gilbert de Clare did not appear then to have inherited Magor he may have acquired part of it as it was also noted earlier that Salisbury seemed to be held from Caerleon. Although there was no bishop of Llandaff until the year after Gilbert's death, these could be the circumstances in which the letter was written, the bishop not becoming involved until after his appointment. There is another possibility however. The boy's mother, Joan, was the daughter of Edward I and her marriage to Gilbert seems to have been part of Edward's determination to end the semi-independent status of the Marcher lords of whom Gilbert was one of the most prominent. Indeed the vacancy at Llandaff was also part of this struggle since Gilbert had tried to assert his right to nominate to the position, a right which Edward would not accept. On Gilbert's marriage to the king's daughter he had had to agree to surrender all his lands to the king and then receive them back to be held jointly with his wife. By so doing he would have to acknowledge that he held the lands from the king, giving up the rights he had claimed as a lord of the March, rights going back to the establishment of the March after the Norman Conquest. After his death therefore the estates and the guardianship of her son would have belonged to Joan until her death in 1307. Joan married a second husband, Ralph de Monthermer, who was allowed to call himself earl of Gloucester and it may therefore be his bailiffs who are referred to in the letter. This arrangement also ceased on Joan's death, although the title was not transferred to her son until the end of the year. The younger Gilbert would still have been under 21 on his mother's death and it may be that the letter relates to this period rather than the earlier one.

Whatever the precise circumstances we can hope that Richard and his parishioners were able to enjoy the produce they had grown. They do seem to have enlisted the bishop to plead their cause, although we don't know whether his efforts were successful.

About a hundred years later, in 1410, Thomas Sledmeir drew up his will, a copy of which was sent for the record to Canterbury as was the custom. In it he is described as '*clerk*', so he had taken some form of religious vows, and '*of the parish of Magor*'. Perhaps he was the village priest, or maybe he only came from Magor. The Canterbury copy of his will survives – in Latin – and in a very difficult to read handwriting so that I have only been able to read a few words here and there. He left money to a number of men described as '*filiolo meo*' which apparently can mean either 'namesake' or 'godson'. Certainly the men so described are all named Thomas so both meanings might apply. Two of them have surnames which are locally known, Thomas Kemmeys and Thomas Herbard (ie Herbert). There is also a mention of John Phillip, vicar of Chepstow. Since Thomas also left money to the churches of Magor and Redwick he clearly had close connections with the village and I think we are justified in seeing him as part of our history.

Later still, in 1563, Matthew Parker, archbishop of Canterbury, required all his bishops to provide details of the parishes within their dioceses. The bishop of Llandaff at the time was Anthony Kitchin, who had been consecrated bishop in

1545 during the reign of Henry VIII, and who had somehow managed to survive all the religious upheavals during the reigns of Henry, Edward VI and Mary and was still at Llandaff when Elizabeth ascended the throne in 1558. Bishop Kitchen managed to complete his return within three weeks, which suggests that the information was already available to him. He was not however able to provide all the information requested. He had been asked for population figures for each parish but explained that he and his officers had not had time to go round to each parish checking with the priest and other inhabitants to find out how many people lived there. There were, of course, no official figures available; the first census did not take place for another 250 years.

The information given in the return is not extensive, just another small fragment of Magor's history. The vicar of Magor in 1563 was called Lawrence Roger; his name is spelt Lawrens in the return. He was resident in his parish and as the ruins adjacent to the churchyard [sometimes called the Procurator's House] are thought to be of a late medieval priest's house built sometime between 1500 and 1550, Lawrence could well have lived there. If so, he had a pretty imposing home of two floors built over a cellar with attics above. There had been an earlier house, probably on this same site, for in 1388, as mentioned earlier, the vicar of Magor paid an annual rent of 6d to Tintern Abbey for 'the rectory by Magor cemetery'. Tintern owned the Church and rectory until the monastery was dissolved in 1536, afterwards they became the property of the earl of Worcester. Either the abbey or the earl could have built the new priest's house, or possibly the incumbent, either Lawrence or one of his predecessors, was responsible. Alternatively it could have been built by one of the local tenants of the abbey. The alterations to the north aisle of the church and the addition of the elaborate porch seem to date to the same period; perhaps the two building projects were related.

Lawrence was not a graduate, but that was not unusual as only five out of approximately 87 clergy listed in the return were. The total appearing in the return is not certain as several men have the same name and it is not always clear whether they are individuals or whether one man held more than one living. No curate is listed for Magor, and as Redwick is listed as a dependant chapel of Magor presumably Lawrence was responsible for both churches.

Two hundred years after Bishop Kitchen reported another bishop of Llandaff set out to collect information on his diocese. Bishop John Ewer was appointed in 1761 and one of his first actions was to send out a questionnaire to all incumbents asking for information on their parishes. The vicar of Magor in 1763 was Richard Vaughan Norman who was also rector of Llanlowell and vicar of Lantrissent. He did not reside in any of his parishes but in a house in Usk called Porth-y-carn which he was to buy in 1775. He also owned Dewstow in Caldicot and was clearly a man of some wealth and position although nothing seems to be known of his origins. Llanlowell and Lantrissent are both easily reached from Usk and Richard served both churches himself. Magor was not so conveniently sited and there he had a curate named David Jones and it was he who completed the return for Magor. David was also the curate at Goldcliffe and its dependant chapel Nash so that, including Redwick, he was responsible for four churches; he was paid £15 a year at Magor and £20 at Goldcliffe. He also kept a school attended by the children of Goldcliffe and Nash. Later in his life he was to be 'Jones of Llangan' a noted preacher and evangelical. David too did not live in Magor; he lived '*in the next parish*' but does not tell us which one, however elsewhere in the return he is said to reside at Goldcliffe. He states that there is no vicarage house. The house which Lawrence Roger may have occupied was probably now a ruin; a manor court of 1738 refers to '*what now remains*' of the '*great house which adjoins the churchyard of Magor*'. David's superior at Goldcliffe, Walter Evans, who completed the return for that parish, was also non-resident living in Pontypool, where he served the chapels at Trevethin and Mamhilad, and he goes into some detail over the reasons why he does not live at Goldcliffe. So much so in fact that he sounds rather defensive, as though he expects to be criticised. He refers to the unhealthiness of the situation which has nearly killed three curates in seven years, although David Jones seems to have survived despite having apparently been at death's door one winter, and Walter adds '*...I and my family are of too sickly and tender a constitution for that country. One winter living there would be our death. I caught the ague once by being there a day and night.*' No doubt he would have regarded Magor with the same distaste; Eighteenth century Pontypool was clearly a much more desirable place of residence.

Note on sources

The letter concerning Richard, vicar of Magor was printed in 'Calendar of Ancient Correspondence concerning Wales', edited by J Goronwy Edwards, 1935, pages 113-114.

The copy of the will of Thomas Sledmeir is held in the National Archive at Kew, reference PROB 11/2A Marche. There is also a brief mention of it in a thesis by J E Hunt 'Monmouthshire wills proved in the prerogative court of Canterbury 1404-1560'.

Bishop Kitchen's report is described in 'Kitchin's return 1563' by J D Evans, in 'Gwent Local History', 1989.

The later report is described in 'The Diocese of Llandaff in 1763' by John R Guy, published by the South Wales Record Society in 1991.

CHAPTER 11

Seaports and Ships

IT HAS already been suggested that transport and trade, in and across the Severn and the Bristol Channel were of considerable importance to Magor from the earliest times. Even though Abergwaitha dwindled in importance and may have disappeared altogether, Magor Pill remained in use as a landing place.

Between 1551 and 1553 Dr Thomas Phaer carried out a survey of all the ports and other landing places around the Welsh coastline. Of Magor he reported that it was '*a pill or creke belonging to Chepstowe*' that is a smaller landing place under the control of the harbour at Chepstow, and like Chepstow it belonged to the earl of Worcester. It is '*in the rulyng of the erle of Worcester whose officers maketh the coquettes and geveth licence*'. A coquette [or cocket] was a document issued by the customs authorities as a warrant that goods were being carried legally, since a wide variety of items could not be moved by ship without a royal licence and the ships had to be able to prove that they were not engaged in smuggling. 'Cocket' is derived from a shortened version of the latin phrase 'quo quietus est' meaning 'by which it is cleared or discharged'. Such warrants had to be paid for and the fact that the documents were being issued by the earl meant that he, rather than the government in London, was collecting the fees. This was another right granted to the original Lords Marcher and clung to by their successors. The government's desire to gain control of this source of revenue may have been one reason for Dr Phaer's survey, together with the need to control the movement of goods and discourage smuggling.

At Magor, Phaer notes that there is '*great lading of small boates with butter, chese and other kyndes of vitelles to shippes*'. The farmers of Magor and the surrounding area obviously produced sufficient surplus to sell in Bristol and probably beyond, since the goods taken by the 'small boats' to 'shippes' were presumably being transferred to larger vessels for their onwards journey. Dr Phaer lived in Pembrokeshire and was himself employed in the customs service there after making his survey. He was also a lawyer and a medical doctor, and seems to have practiced both professions. He also found time to write books on the law and on medicine, to write poetry and to start making the first translation of Virgil's Aeneid into English although he died before he was able to complete it.

Nearly a hundred years after Dr Phaer made his survey another customs officer recorded in his 'letterbook' copies of correspondence and memoranda written mostly in connection with his work. John Byrd was probably born in Bristol but he married a girl from a long established South Wales family, the Says, and accumulated property in Newport and Caerleon. His letterbook covers 1648 to 1680 with gaps, and gives a good picture of the period. Although Magor does not really feature in the book there are a couple of useful references. In one letter addressed to his superiors he lists all the ports under the authority of Cardiff and although the list does not include Magor it does include Redcliffe Pill which, if it is not an alternative name for the same place, must have been in much the same area as Phaer's Magor Pill. In another letter dated 1649, Byrd mentions having seized tobacco from Barbados '*which was privately landed at Redwick*' and asks for permission to release it to the sailors who own it provided they pay the customs and excise fees due.

In the same letter there is a reference to accusations that butter was being exported direct from South Wales rather than going through Bristol, whose merchants had a monopoly on two thirds of Welsh butter exports. This seems to have been a longstanding dispute involving the government, the city of Bristol and the merchants but the farmers, the producers of the butter, do not appear to have had any say in the matter. The production of butter, and probably other dairy products, for trade through Bristol, is obviously still as important as it was one hundred years earlier.

There is a reference in Byrd's letter to '*some very smale botes which we knowe do constantly trade for Englande*' which recalls Phaer's '*small boats*'. Some of these no doubt used Magor Pill both for legitimate trade and also for any smuggling they could get away with.

Bristol was a major port used by seagoing ships from all parts of the world as well as being a centre for local trade from the west of England and south Wales. Not all the ships reached their destination however. In 1393 John Banberye of Bristol petitioned the House of Commons for help in connection with a ship of his, wrecked in the Severn. The ship had sailed from Gascony, most probably from Bordeaux, which was still under the English crown at this time, laden with wine and other goods but it went aground near Goldcliffe. Before John and his men could do anything to save the ship and its cargo numbers of men, three to four hundred if John is not exaggerating, came from the whole area between Newport and Chepstow, broke open the ship with hatchets and carried off not only the cargo but also all the ship's gear. Magor is mentioned as one of the places from which the men came. The Commons gave such help as they could, including letters to the lords in whose lordships the men lived demanding that they be forced to make restitution, but I don't know whether this was successful. It is possible that the lords believed that as lords Marcher they had the right to wrecks off their lands. Certainly the Tintern charters stated '*they shall have wreck of sea and liberty of fish up to the middle of Severn opposite the lands of the abbot and monks*', and as late as the reign of James I the earl of Worcester was involved in cases in which he claimed his rights to wrecks in the Severn and the Wye.

Two separate discoveries of the remains of ships near Magor have added further to our knowledge of the water-borne trade of the area. The earlier of the two, mentioned in chapter 2, was found at Barlands Farm, not far from the site of the very early cattle sheds also already noted. The construction of the boat fits the Romano-Celtic style of boat-building of the first three centuries AD, and as mentioned it has been dated by dendrochronology to AD 283-301. Similar craft have been found in London and also in Europe. It had been used to reinforce the bank of a creek that at one time flowed up to that point and possibly formed part of a quay. Prior to its reuse in this way it would probably have traded in the estuary as we have seen in the examples considered above. The other boat was retrieved, with great difficulty, from the mud of the Severn at Magor Pill, and timbers from it have been dated to 1240, although it had seen much use since it was built as there was evidence of repairs to the hull. At the time it sank it was carrying a cargo of iron ore. Although neither boat necessarily traded out of Abergwaitha similar craft would no doubt have done so when it was a flourishing port. Such evidence for local trade on the Severn suggests that it remained important for Magor from Roman times or earlier and throughout the existence of Abergwaitha. Even after the latter ceased to exist, and as we have seen it was said to be deserted in the Inquisition of John Meriet in 1327, the evidence of Thomas Phaer and John Byrd shows that its site remained in use as a landing place for several centuries.

Note on sources

Dr Thomas Phaer's report on the harbours and customs administration of Wales under Edward VI by W R B Robinson. Bulletin of the Board of Celtic Studies, 1971-72.

The Letter-Book of John Byrd, Customs Collector in South-East Wales 1648-80. Edited by S K Roberts. South Wales Record Society, 1999.

John Banberye's petition is included in the 'Calendar of Ancient Petitions relating to Wales', edited by W Rees, 1975.

Barland's Farm, Magor, Gwent: a Romano-Celtic boat. Nigel Nayling etc. Antiquity September 1994.

The Magor Pill Medieval Wreck. Nigel Nayling CBA Research Report 115, 1998.

CHAPTER 12

A Magor Farmer

IN APRIL 1591, as Edward Thomas lay seriously ill at his home in Magor, his friends gathered around to witness his will. Probably also present would have been his servants and farm workers for Edward was a prosperous dairy farmer. His wife, I think, may have died earlier for there is no mention of her in his will, but his four young children; his son Giles and his daughters Bridget, Elizabeth and Margaret, none of them yet of age, would also have been there. He had obviously given some thought to his will since it is quite detailed and includes bequests to over thirty individuals. Over fifty cattle are listed together with horses and pigs, also various amounts of grain and household items. This suggests prosperity and a certain status as also does the fact that he asks to be buried in the chancel of Magor church, a privilege reserved for people of some standing in the community.

His first bequests were of a charitable nature, money for Magor church and the cathedral of Llandaff, together with two shillings *'for forgotten tithes'*, and ten shillings for the repair of the road *'in the common between Magor mill and the Dynche hill'*. Mill common and Dinch hill are names still current so that we know more or less where this road lay. Possibly Edward used the road regularly and was well aware of its need of repair. Road repair was the responsibility of the parish in which the road lay and charitable donations towards the cost were common in wills at this period.

The land mentioned in the will is all held on lease, except possibly for the small piece of ground which he left to John Morgan. On it John was to build a house which was leased to him for three lives, his own and that of his wife and one of his children. Leases were commonly made for three lives, that is three people were named and the lease continued through their lives until the last of the three died.

If Edward had any other land of his own it may have been settled on his son in a separate manner. His son, Giles, receives *'the leases of all my houses and lands which I hold of Mr Kemes of Kemes'*. This was probably Edward Kemeys who lived at Kemeys Inferior before moving to Bertholey and who died in 1622. No details are given of the sites of these properties but there is one possible clue.

After several generations the Kemeys heiress married a Mr Colthurst Bateman and on the 1847 Tithe map a homestead owned by Colthurst Bateman is shown next to the Wheatsheaf Inn, the building now known as Manor farm. Part of the present building is said to be of 16th century date and might therefore have been part of Edward Thomas's home, although there is, of course, no way of knowing whether this is in fact where he lived.

One of Edward's daughters, Bridget, received *'the lease of the house and three ferendells of land which I had from Sir Thomas Revett'*. Sir Thomas lived at Penhow, which he had bought in 1567, and owned land in Magor and Redwick. A *'ferendell'* is a quarter of an acre. The other two daughters, Elizabeth and Margaret, together with their brother Giles, were left money to purchase [that is purchase the leases of] *'certain lands of my lord of Worcester during their natural lives successively'*, presumably everyone knew which lands were meant.

Edward left money to his family. To his sister, Anne, he left 40 shillings *'which is in her own hand'*, presumably he had already given the money to her. To his brother James he left *'all the sum of money which he owes me'*, it seems that Edward was subsidising his family. James also received two colts and his other brother, Jevan, had £3 in money and one colt. A colt was also bequeathed to Edward Kemeys and each of the children received a mare. It seems likely that Edward bred horses since the will mentions a nag, five mares and eight colts, a total of fourteen. Two of the colts are described as 'stoned' that is they were complete horses, not geldings.

Although Edward was a dairy farmer none of his cattle seem to have been left to his son, although it is possible that there were more than he actually lists in the will and that the remainder went to Giles. Most of the cattle listed were left to his daughters, each receiving ten cows, three calves and three other beasts. His bequest to his servant, Elizabeth was just *'a cow'* with no details given but other bequests were more specific, for example Maude John was to have *'the first cow that shall calve'* whereas Edward Richard had a *'heifer of three years old which will calve before Lammas tide'*. Lammas is at the beginning of August. Edward does not seem to have kept sheep, at least none are mentioned in the will, but he did have pigs which were to be divided equally between his daughters, except for *'four of the best to be fattened for the provision of the house'*, the house being presumably the household established for his children.

Most of his *'household stuff'* is divided between his daughters but certain items, probably the most valuable, are mentioned specifically. Each of the four children was to receive a bedstead together with a feather bed, except for Bridget who had a flock bed instead, that is one stuffed with rags etc. rather than feathers, presumably Edward only had three feather beds. Each also had a bolster and a *'helling'*, or bedspread. The three girls had six pairs of sheets each and Giles had two pairs. It would appear that at this period a bed and bedding were something of a status symbol for twenty-five years after this, in 1616, William Shakespeare was to leave his second-best bed to his wife. Pewter too was probably a sign of status, not of so high a level as silver but very few people would have been able to afford silver. Each of Edward's daughters was to receive six pieces of pewter and Giles was to have the rest. Each of the four children was also to have '*a crock and pan*', there are no further details but I think these may have been for use in the dairy, for the preparation or storage of cream, butter or cheese. The number of cows, described as '*milch kine*', and calves listed in the will suggest that Edward's main interest was in dairy farming. There is mention of suckling calves and weaning calves and also of a heifer in calf and the first cow to calve. However he probably also reared some of the calves for beef since a total of thirteen steers is mentioned. There were also two bulls one of which was left to his daughter Elizabeth. The other was left to the executors of the will '*for the provision of my said children*'. I'm not sure what this means, possibly it was to ensure the continuation of the herd, and therefore the dairy farm, so as to provide for the children until they were old enough to look after themselves. Forty years earlier Dr Phaer had described the small boats which carried butter and cheese from Magor Pill to Bristol and no doubt similar craft carried the produce of Edward Thomas's farm across the Severn.

It is not clear whether he also grew crops; certainly his bequests include a fairly large amount of grain. Either a bushel or half a bushel, mostly of wheat but including one bushel of barley, are left to ten separately named people. A bushel of wheat contained 60 pounds and a bushel of barley 47 pounds. Also he left his '*wain*' to Giles, a large cart which could have been used for carrying corn and possibly hay for the animals.

The children were left in the care of Lewes Rawlinge, who was also executor of the will. Jane and Johane Rawlinge also appear in the will but we do not know their relationship to Lewes, although I guess they may have been his wife and daughter. If so this may explain why the children were left in his care, rather than that of Edward's brothers or sister, since there is no evidence from the will that the latter were married, or of how old they were. Johane's bequest is interesting, she was to receive four cows and two heifers, three pairs of sheets, and money '*to buy her household stuff*', and it is possible that this was to form part of her dowry when she married. Lewes was also left a couple of oxen which had probably been used for haulage; I'm not sure why they did not go with the wain to Giles. The overseers of the will were Edward's two brothers, together with Walter Hopkins and Edward Kemeys.

Edward's will is a further example of the importance of the pasturelands of Magor for the farmers of the village and as we have seen, the rearing of cattle dates back to the earliest times.

Note on sources

A copy of the will of Edward Thomas is held in the Public Record Office, catalogue reference: PROB/11/77 and it has been printed in 'Monmouthshire Wills 1560-1601' by Judith Jones, published by the South Wales Record Society in 1997.

CHAPTER 13

Nonconformist Gentlemen

FIFTY YEARS after Edward Thomas made his bequests another will mentioning Magor was being proved. William Wroth became rector of Llanvaches in 1611 but gradually his dislike of the changes in the Church made by Archbishop Laud grew and in 1639 he resigned his living and set up at Llanvaches the first non-conformist chapel in Wales. He died in 1641 and in his will he left:

> '*three acres of lands in the parish of Magor which I have purchased of Edmund Herbert of Penhow and Blanche his wife, to uses expressed, the rents to be divided on the first of April between twelve of the poorest people in the parish of Llanvaches*'.

The responsibility for carrying out his wishes was given to Henry Walter who is described in the will as '*Henry Walter of St Brides, preacher of God's word*'. Henry was a local man as his mother was a daughter of John Robnet of St Brides and she had married John Walter of Piercefield near Chepstow. The land continued to be used for the benefit of the poor of Llanvaches since in 1707 a manorial survey noted that:

> '*the poor of Llanvaches hold in the parish of Magor ... four acres of land being heretofore the lands of Edmund Herbert ...*' and even later, at the time of the Tithe Apportionment in 1846, the Churchwardens of Llanvaches held four acres in Magor, most likely the same land bequeathed by William Wroth over two hundred years earlier. The land is described as meadow and lay on the lower lands near Greenmoor.

Henry Walter was one of the young men attracted to Llanvaches by the growing reputation of Wroth, as was another Monmouthshire nonconformist, Walter Cradock. Both of them were known to John Byrd the customs officer we met in chapter 11, and are mentioned in his 'letterbook'. Indeed Walter Cradock is referred to as Byrd's *'loving friend and neighbour'*. William Wroth died before the Civil War began, but his associates continued his work at Llanvaches until the progress of the war made this impossible. Together with members of their congregation they took refuge first in Bristol, and then, in 1643, in London at the church of All Hallows the Great. Both Henry and Walter were included in the list of itinerant ministers appointed to preach in South Wales in 1646. Henry was a minister in Newport from 1653 until the Restoration, and Walter at Llangwm from 1655 to his death in 1659.

It was from this same church of All Hallows that Thomas Barnes was sent to Wales 'to preach the Gospel', although whether he had previously been connected with the Henry Walter / Walter Cradock group is not recorded. I have found no information on his origins; it is possible that he too was a local man and would thus have been familiar with the area, but if not he could have gained useful information from the Welsh refugees at All Hallows. It is not clear either exactly when he was sent to Wales. John Edwards who held the living from 1635 was apparently ejected from it before 1649 and replaced by Morgan Jones who was in turn ejected at some time after 1650 when presumably Thomas Barnes took over.

At the Restoration, although Morgan Jones returned to Magor, non-conformity remained strong in the area and Thomas Barnes continued to serve those who shared his views, moving around and preaching in private houses although both preacher and the owner of the house where the meeting was held faced heavy fines if they were caught. There were of course always people ready to report on the activities of their neighbours and in 1669 it was said that meetings were being held in Magor 'at the house of Mr Samuel Jones of Little Salisbury'.

I am not sure whether 'Little Salisbury' was just a part of what is now Salisbury Farm or whether it was an alternative name for the property. Mr Samuel Jones is mentioned in a will of 1654 where he is described as 'of Salisbury' but ten years later in 1664 the will of Cecil Watkins mentions her nephew Samuel Jones 'of Little Salisbury' and it is possible that the two are the same as the person in whose home these meetings were held.

Another participant in the meetings at Little Salisbury was William Millman, who had earlier been a schoolmaster in Magor. In 1649/50 the 'Act for the better Propagation and Preaching of The Gospel in Wales' was passed. It was this act which led to the appointment of itinerant preachers in Wales, including Walter Cradock and Henry Walter as already noted. Another provision was a grant to establish schools to *'banish ignorance and profaneness amongst the young'*. Sixty-three schools were to be established in the major market towns and in Monmouthshire these were at Monmouth, Usk, Chepstow, Newport and Magor. It is perhaps surprising to find Magor regarded as a 'major market town' on a par with Monmouth and the other three towns; clearly it was regarded as a place of some importance at this period.

William Millman was appointed schoolmaster at Magor in 1650 at an annual salary of £40. However the Act which set up the schools came up for reconsideration in 1653 and was not renewed, so it is likely that the school did not last for very long. We do not know where William held his school but it may have been in the room over the church porch since a school was in existence there in 1834 when the churchwardens paid 5 shillings for a grate for the schoolroom. There is a later reference to *'Haddock the schoolmaster at Magor'* who in about 1780 was a local Baptist leader but after so long a gap this is probably a separate development. Again we don't know where he held his school, there was a school later in the chapel but this was not built until 1816. Meetings before this were held in private houses, as they had been in 1669, and so the school was probably also held in someone's home. Millman, like Thomas Barnes, remained in Monmouthshire after the Restoration and was apparently still at work in 1690.

Walter Cradock's daughter, Lois, married Richard Creed who had held positions of some importance under the Commonwealth. These he lost at the Restoration and he eventually joined his father-in-law in Monmouthshire. Richard's brother John, proved rather more adaptable to the new conditions and remained at the Admiralty where he was the friend, and rival, of his colleague Samuel Pepys. In 1655 Richard Creed witnessed an agreement by which Walter Cradock was to lease, for £50 *'all that decayed house and barn at Magor called Moore Grange'*. The agreement was with Oliver Cromwell, who had been granted the lands of the earl of Worcester, the latter having been one of the most faithful supporters of Charles I.

However, it is probable that the lease did not take effect as in another source Moore Grange is said to have been leased by Cromwell to Edward Herbert whose ancestor had been steward there for Tintern Abbey. However when the heir of the earl of Worcester announced his conversion to protestantism in 1650 Cromwell returned at least some of the estates that had been confiscated from his father, and possibly Moore Grange was included.

Magor also makes a fleeting appearance in the life of a later nonconformist gentleman. In October 1741 John Wesley was to meet Hywel Harris at Wilcrick but was late arriving having had to wait for a boat at the New Passage. Finding no-one at Wilcrick, his diary records that *'...we went back to Magor and thence in the morning to Llanmartin...'*. Unfortunately he did not record where he stayed or who with, nor whether he met any of the Magor people during his brief visit. Again we have only a fragment of information, and none of the details we would like to have.

Note on sources
Information in this chapter is taken from the 'History of the Puritan Movement in Wales', 1920 by Thomas Richards; also from 'History of Protestant Nonconformity in Wales' 1861 by Thomas Rees and from Sir Joseph Bradney's 'History of Monmouthshire'.

CHAPTER 14

A Manorial Survey

IN SEPTEMBER 1707 Queen Anne was in the sixth year of her reign and the country was – yet again – at war with France. The Duke of Marlborough was mid-way through his series of great battles; Blenheim and Ramillies were already won, Oudenarde and Malplaquet yet to come. However in Magor life continued as usual and on September 30th Mordecai Jones, steward of the court of the Manor of Magor and Redwick le Green Moor, together with a jury composed of six tenants of the manor, listened as the bailiff, Thomas Stedder, worked through his rent roll giving details of the tenants of the manor and the rents due from each.

It was known that the manor had once been much larger but that at some time in the past it had been divided into three parts. The part for which this court was being held belonged to John Morgan and the other two parts, which held their own courts, currently belonged to Edward Kemeys and George Jones. John Morgan, who is called 'of London' is probably the John Morgan known as 'the Merchant', who retired to Rhiwpperra after making his fortune in London and who died in 1715. Edward Kemeys is probably the great-grandson of the Edward who was a friend of Edward Thomas the farmer of chapter 12. This later Edward died in 1710. The third lord of the manor, George Jones, is probably the George Jones of Magor who died in 1743 but might be George Jones of Little Salisbury. In chapter 13 we saw that nonconformist meetings were being held at Little Salisbury, then the home of Mr Samuel Jones, in 1669. George is likely to be of the same family, even a direct descendent, but it is not possible to be sure as there were too many Joneses around.

The details of the earlier manor and its division may no longer have been remembered but the individual properties involved were still known. However, as the jury stated, they were:

'so intermixed with other mannors that we cannot set forth the bounds and limits of the same'.

This is borne out by the details given in the rent roll, where there are many holdings of only one or two acres scattered throughout the manor. There are some larger holdings but most are small and are held by a number of different people. Some of these people would also hold land from other landlords; from Edward Kemeys and George Jones in the other parts of what had once been one manor, or in other manors, for even when joined together this one did not include all the land in Magor and Redwick. In Magor, for example there was all the land formerly owned by Tintern Abbey and now belonging to the Duke of Beaufort. In Redwick we know of the manor of Raglan, alternatively known as Dennis Court, which at this period was held by Thomas Lewis of St Pierre. Apart from holding this manor in Redwick he is listed in our survey as also holding three acres there, no doubt a convenient addition to his main holding but on its own no indication that he was a major landowner in the area.

Although the land held by each tenant is listed there is, unfortunately, not enough detail given for us to be able to identify it. Most of the locations are in the form 'bordered by the land of A, B, C and D on the north, south, east and west'. However in a few cases the information does allow us to relate it, at least in part, to the present day village. In Magor there are three properties listed as next to each other. One was a barn held by George Pranch, at a rent of nine shillings a year. He almost certainly held other property as well as he was the vicar of Magor and also of Llanwern, Undy and Goldcliffe. His father Richard had also been vicar of Magor and also of Undy and Llanfihangell Rogiet. George was an educated man, having attended Jesus College, Oxford, and had married a local girl. His wife, Elizabeth, was the daughter of John Irish of Magor whose occupation is given as '*scrivener*', that is someone who could draw up documents in proper form for other people.

That such a specialist should be based in Magor suggests that it was still a major local centre. After Elizabeth's death George married another local girl, the daughter of the vicar of Mathern. Next to George's barn was a house whose tenant was a widow named Mary Francis, she had only the house with no land although she may have held land elsewhere. Next to Mary's house was an orchard, held by William Stedder, one of the boundaries of which was '*the lane from Magor Cross towards Wentwood*'. Another boundary in the survey is described as '*the highway from Magor to Wentwood*' but we cannot be sure whether these are two different roads or alternative descriptions of the same one. The 'highway' is probably the road we have already met before as a possible Roman road, and as '*the way leading from Aberweytha towards Wentwood*' in the Wentwood Survey, and is today represented by Bowdens Lane to the north of the village and by Whitewall to the south. Whitewall also occurs as a boundary within the manor, and other names which still exist are Blackwall, Westend ('*westendtown*'), Rushwall, Pool y ffarn Reen, Sea Street, Windmill Reen, Broadmead and Toadmead. Some of these names have also appeared in other chapters.

In the survey the manor is divided between demesne land and the rest of the manor. Originally the demesne was land reserved for the lord's own use, but gradually it became usual to lease it out in the same way as the rest of the property. The demesne land is still listed separately in this survey but the only apparent difference is that tenants of demesne land do not owe suit of court, that is they are not under the jurisdiction of the manor court. However since the court apparently no longer deals with anything other than the leases this probably made little difference. In the Abbey court of More Grange in 1493 we saw tenants being fined for failing to repair property but there is nothing like this in 1707. In the survey there is a reference to demesne lands let at 'rack rent'. This term did not then have the derogatory sense it has since gained, and refers to rent paid by those holding by annual tenancies and where the landlord was responsible for repairs so that the manor court would not be involved.

Except in one case no details are given of the leases, only an annual rent. I am not sure whether the leases were re-negotiated annually, or the rent re-assessed or possibly both. The exception is a considerable property leased to Edmund Rosser. The lease is for eleven years and started on the 2nd February 1697 and would therefore run out the year following the survey. The property consisted of a house, described as a 'Mantion House' together with a barn, an orchard, and fourteen acres of land. Actually he may not have rented the whole of the house as the full description is *'that part of the Mantion house which belongs to the lord of this manor'*. In another document a little later than this, in 1738, there is a reference to *'the Great House which adjoins the Churchyard of Magor [which] does belong to the Lords of Greenmoor'*. This 'Great House', which is surely the so called 'Procurators House' whose ruins are still visible, must, I think, be the 'Mantion House' part of which was leased to Edmund Rosser. He also held, listed separately from this and so presumably not part of the lease, two burgages, a *'little barn or tye house'*, and another nine acres.

Another large property, a *'messuage or dwelling house'* and twenty-two acres was held by Charles Jones 'of the Foorde', so named to distinguish him from the numerous other Joneses living in the area, and deriving from the family's connection with the property at Langstone still called Ford Farm. The Magor property had previously been held by his father, Robert, and is described as lying *'along or near to the river or brook which runneth from Salisbury to Magor'*. This is, for once, an identifiable location for Salisbury Farm and the brook running past it to Magor are still there. The survey adds that the property is *'commonly called Red Moor'*. This is not, I think, a name now used but I think it must relate to the farm called Castel Coch, ie Red Castle, a name which is referred to in 1314 as we saw in looking at the Survey of Wentwood. In the Tithe Apportionment of 1847 there is a reference to *'Red Moor and Castel Coch'*. It is possible therefore that Castel Coch is the *'messuage or dwelling house'* held by Charles Jones.

A smaller property was held by a widow, Elizabeth Jones, who rented a house and garden, a barn, and ½ an acre of land for which she paid 10 shillings a year and *'a couple of hens'*. This is the only example in the survey of rent being paid in kind rather than money and even here it is in addition to a money rent. The hens might be an outdated relic of an earlier age but possibly Elizabeth preferred to retain at least a little of the traditional payment. Alternatively it may have been easier for her to find hens than extra cash.

We had above a reference to 'the lords of Greenmoor', and the full title of the manor was 'Magor, Redwick and le Greenmoor'. The lords of Greenmoor were the three men who held parts of what had once been one manor, quite possibly that which in 1327, was inherited by John Meriet's wife, Mary, as we saw in chapter 6, and which included *'a pasture called le Grenemore'*. Mary Meriet had a fourth part of the manor, probably there had been further rearrangement of the parts of the manor since the fourteenth century, but its original unity was still remembered. Greenmoor was a large area of common pasture to the west of Magor and the name can still be seen on today's maps. It was not part of the parish of Magor and did not in fact lie within any parish. The tenants of the lord of Greenmoor had the right to pasture their beasts on the moor, but so also did the inhabitants of Bishton, Llandevenny and Wilcrick, villages which also adjoined the moor, although they had to pay one shilling and four pence annually to the lords of the manor for the right to do so. Moreover the lord of the manor had the right to round up all the cattle on the moor during May and any animals whose owners did not have the right to pasture them there would become the property of the lord of the manor and their owners would be fined. As we saw in connection with Wentwood, common land was not common to everyone, only to those who had rights there.

Thomas Stedder, the bailiff of the manor, also held land there although it was only one acre in Redwick. However he too held other lands apart from this. His will of 1726 mentions an estate in Redwick which belonged to his late wife which is to be sold to pay his debts and provide for his younger children, and a tenement in Magor which he left to his daughter Ann. The family home at Talgarth was left to his son Thomas.

This survey shows that much remained from earlier times, and although the people might change some names do continue, as also do the place names and the uses made of the land.

Note on sources
This manorial survey is in the Gwent Record Office, reference D668.25, in a volume of copy surveys. Additional information on the people mentioned is mostly taken from Bradney's History.

... and then

THE HISTORY of Magor does not, of course, come to an end in 1707 but I decided to end this account here. From the eighteenth century onwards information becomes more plentiful as comparatively more documents have survived, in part because more were produced. There are also the beginnings of official, government produced, material which tends to be filed and kept. Parish Registers become more common although they had been made compulsory in 1538 and the first census took place in 1801. With so much more information available it seemed better to keep the later history for a separate publication – or publications!

Although the various documents I have described here do not form a consecutive account of the history of the village there is a perhaps surprising amount of continuity in the account. Some themes recur throughout. One of the most obvious is farming and particularly the pasturing of dairy herds. From the very earliest times this has featured as an important part of the economy of the area, from the bronze age cattle sheds through the boats carrying butter and cheese across the Severn and the milch cows belonging to Edward Thomas to the cattle on Greenmoor in 1707 and on, indeed, to the present day. Another is the importance of links, for trade and travel, across the Severn to Bristol and beyond. Magor's port at Abergwaitha may have disappeared but its function is continued by the rail link through the tunnel and by the two road bridges.

Another constant is the general shape of the village, with its centre around the church which has been in place at least eight centuries, and the outlying farms amidst their fields. Some of the names of these farms are still those of the earliest records such as Salisbury and Castel Coch recorded in the 14th century. Others, such as Merthyrgerin and Moor which go back to the 12th century, remain in the old locations although the names have changed. Much else has changed of course but even modern buildings are affected by history to some extent since they either replace a predecessor or their position may have to respect the existence of other earlier buildings. I do not want to over-emphasize this continuity but clearly our village does have a history, some of which I have described in this account, and the events of that history have helped to produce the village of today.

Appendix on Placenames

Magor – the placename

The name 'Magor' or 'Magwyr' in the Welsh spelling, is generally accepted as deriving from the Latin *maceria* which means 'masonry wall' although it seems later to have developed the meanings 'building remains' or 'ancient ruins'. In the book by Osbourne and Hobbs on the placenames of Eastern Gwent, they give the meaning as 'walls or enclosure used of ruins'. The word also occurs in other languages and Oliver Padel in his book on Cornish placename elements gives the old Cornish word *magoer* with the meaning 'wall, probably in the sense ruins or remains'. He also gives the related words *magwyr* (Welsh), *moger* (Breton), *macoer* (Old Breton), and *magoaerou* (Middle Breton, plural).

The derivation of the name seems clear enough but it is much less obvious why the name should have been given to the village of Magor in Gwent. The earliest written reference to the village is apparently around 1153, but presumably it had existed for some time before that. It is possible that Magor was one of the 'villae' listed in the Gloucestershire Domesday as being 'in Wales' but this cannot be proved. It seems reasonable however to suppose that the village was named by the time of the arrival of the Normans, and therefore to suggest that the ruins or remains after which it was named were Roman or Romano-British since there would have been little building in stone in the intervening period.

I have thought of four possibilities for the source of the name, but there may well be others.

a. There might have been a Roman building of some kind, perhaps a villa belonging to one of the local dignitaries at Caerwent or possibly something connected with the military base at Caerleon.
b. There might be some connection with the hill-fort at Wilcrick, though this is perhaps less likely to have had associations with masonry walls.
c. It might refer to sea defences erected by the Romans along the Severn where there was a port associated with Magor up to the 14th century.
d. The stream that runs from the St Brides valley through Magor to the Severn may have been embanked or canalised where it runs through the marshland between the village and the Severn and/or there might have been a causeway

leading from the village to the port. This area is still known as Whitewall, which is suggestive. There is also a Blackwall and it may be that the 'white' wall was constructed of stone and the 'black' wall of earth.

Magor does not seem to occur very frequently as a place name. I have traced only a few in Wales. In Gwent there is a farm near Wolvesnewton called Cwm-Vagor or Cwmfagor. There are also references, dating back apparently to 1319, to 'a field called Magor' or 'field Magor' in the parish of Llanfihangel Rogiet. I think this may be in the area where the remains of a Roman building were discovered in 1996.

In Ceredigion there is Abermagwyr, which is on the Afon Ystwyth, inland from Aberystwyth. Here there has been the exciting discovery recently of what may be a hitherto unknown Roman Villa. A magetometer survey has revealed a typical villa plan, and it is hoped that excavation will provide more information (The discovery was reported in Current Archaeology March 2010). There is also a Clwyd y Fagor in Glamorgan.

There are two examples of the placename in Cornwall, given by Padel. The first of these is Magor Farm near Illogan. This is particularly interesting as Roman remains were discovered there in 1931. This was the first (and, I think, only) Roman structure to have been discovered in Cornwall. The other occurrence is Maker (this name apparently has the same derivation as Magor), near Mt Edgecombe.

Magor, in the forms Magoer and Magoar also occurs as a place name in Brittany.

Some other names

1 Salisbury – the name of this farm dates back to at least 1314 when it appears in the inquisitio post mortem of Gilbert de Clare, but I do not know how it came to be so called, or whether it has any connection with the city of Salisbury in Wiltshire. A possible link is through William Marshall the elder whose mother was the sister of Patrick, earl of Salisbury.

2 Merthyr Gerin – Merthyr started as a term connected with the commemoration of Martyrs, but seems to have developed a more general sense as a memorial to someone locally venerated. Gerin, presumably the person so commemorated, is a form of the name Geraint but we do not know who he was. There are numerous Geraints in literature, one or two were probably historical personages, but most inhabit the worlds of myth and legend. Merthyr Gerin was the name of one of the abbey granges in Magor belonging to Tintern Abbey and later became known as Upper Grange Farm. Lower Grange farm, originally Moor Grange, was the other abbey grange.

3 Castel Coch – that is Red Castle. There is an outcrop of reddish coloured rock on the north side of the M4 quite near to the present day farm. There is also a later name 'red moor' also probably nearby.

4 Warn Arrow – I am not a Welsh speaker, but I think this name comes from Gwaun, a noun meaning moor or meadow together with the adjective Garw, meaning coarse or rough. If I have understood the rules of mutation correctly this would become Y Warn Arw. The farm name is sometimes given as Warn Harrow.

5 Skeviot – the comments in section four apply here also. I think the name comes from Ysgeifiog, a placename meaning the place of elder trees, of which there are several examples in Wales. 'Ysg' sounds like and is often written as 'sk'; for example Skirrid from Ysgyrid or Skenfrith from Ynysgynwraidd.

6 Abergwaitha – 'aber' is a common element of Welsh placenames meaning 'mouth' as of a river, stream etc. Gwaith means 'work', and in this name probably refers to the embanked Whitewall stream which here joins the Severn.

Magor – *not* **the placename** (with thanks to Google)

In Hebrew a word which can be transliterated as Magor means fear or terror. In the book of Jeremiah chapter 20 the prophet says to Pashur the priest, who had put him in the stocks, "The Lord hath not called thy name Pashur but Magor-missabib". This means something like 'terror on every side'.

In Hungarian legend the brothers Hunor and Magor, whilst out hunting, followed a magical white stag which led them to a land where they married two princesses. Hunor became the founding father of the Huns and Magor of the Magyars.

There is an Italian cheese called Magor. It is formed from alternating layers of *ma*scarpone and *gor*gonzola; it is alternatively known as Gormas.